Quick guide to

MP3 and Digital Music

Ian Waugh

PC Publishing

PC Publishing
Export House
130 Vale Road
Tonbridge
Kent TN9 1SP
UK

Tel 01732 770893
Fax 01732 770268
email info@pc-publishing.co.uk
website http://www.pc-publishing.co.uk

First published 2000

ISBN 1 870775 67 8

British Library Cataloguing in Publication Data
A catalogue record for this book is available from the British Library

Printed in Great Britain by Martins the Printers Limited

Contents

Preface

Never has a development had such an effect on an industry as MP3 has had on the music business. Cries of 'revolution' are not exaggerated and as we head into the third Millennium we are seeing new methods of music promotion and distribution which were simply not possible before MP3.

More and more bands and musicians are making use of the technology to promote awareness of their music, and an increasing number of people are becoming musicians thanks to easy-to-use music creation software. But it's not just newcomers who are using MP3. Well-established artists are using the Web and MP3 to promote and sell their music– and even give it away.

And it's all out there on the Web, waiting for you to listen to and download. You can listen to the files not only on your computer but on portable MP3 players, on your hi fi and even in the car.

But as with anything new, MP3 is not without its detractors and the music industry has not welcomed it with open arms. The availability of MP3 files on the Web has opened up again the whole copyright and piracy can of worms.

This book will provide you with a Quick Guide to all things MP3. It covers all the essential elements and tells you everything you need to know to make full use of this new technology.

Dedication

To my Mother and Father,

...who played a most essential part in the production of this book ...

With much love

MP3 essentials

S urf over to www.searchterms.com and you'll see a Top 100 list of words that people search for when surfing the Net. You can bet that 'sex' will be up there near the top – unless the Government has been putting bromide in the water – but you can also bet that 'MP3' will be up there, too, and it's not uncommon to see MP3 with an even higher ranking than sex. Quite what this says about the interests and priorities of surfers we leave for the sociologists to discuss. But clearly there is massive interest in MP3s so let's see what all the fuss is about.

What is MP3?

MP3 is a compressed audio file format. That's it! It's a little like Zip files on the PC and Stuffit files on the Mac in that it reduces the size of the original file. However, there are a couple of important differences as we'll see in the next chapter.

MP3 stands for MPEG 1 Audio Layer 3. Don't let your mate tell you it stands for MPEG 3 'cause it doesn't – in fact, MPEG 3 doesn't exist! Let's see what it all means.

MPEG is an acronym for Moving Picture Experts Group, a group of industry boffins set up under the auspices of the ISO (International Standards Organisation) to develop standards for video, audio, graphics and so on.

The group began in 1988 and developed MPEG 1, which includes MP3, and the standard was approved in 1992. Four years later we start to see MP3 software appearing. Yes, like a good bottle of vino, these things take time.

MPEG can compress video, audio or both. The audio compression element was developed by the Fraunhofer Institut Integrierte Schaltungen of Germany (normally just called Fraunhofer ISS) in three parts or layers.

There are many ways to compress an audio file (we get into this in more detail in the next chapter) and the three layers use increasingly sophisticated levels of compression. When the format was devised, it took a state-of-the-art computer to decompress layer 3 while layers 1 and 2 could be decompressed more easily by computers of the day. But what was state-of-the-art then is very old technology now and all modern computers have no trouble at all decompressing layer 3 files.

So, put all the bits together and you get MPEG 1 Audio Layer 3 which was shortened to MP3.

Take a peek

For more information about what people search for on the Web, take a look at: www.searchenginewatch.com/facts/searches.html

What happened to MPEG 3?

An MPEG 3 standard was developed but it was merged with MPEG 2. (MPEG is pronounced em-peg).

MIDI

Musical Instrument Digital Interface, a standard for transferring music instructions between keyboards, sound modules and sequencers. Not something we look at in this book.

MPEG links

There are hundred so pages of information about MPEG on the Web. Type MPEG into a search engine and stand well back! Here are a couple to get you started:
www.cselt.it/mpeg
www.mpeg.org

The forgotten compressor

Thomson Multimedia of the USA also had a hand in developing the MP3 audio compression system but is usually forgotten when the credits are being handed out. Most folks who have cause to refer to the audio compression format refer to it as the Fraunhofer format to distinguish it from other MP3 compression systems, more of which in Chapter 2.

Other MPEGs

For the insatiably curious, here's a little information about the other MPEG formats.

MPEG 2 builds on MPEG 1 by adding support for five channels of surround sound plus a low frequency channel for sub woofers. It also supports lower sample rates of 16, 22.05 and 24kHz and a bit rate of 8kbps.

Bits and rates

kHz: Kilohertz (thousands of cycles per second), used to measure sample rates.

kbps: Kilobits (or thousands of bits) per second, used to measure transfer rates.

MPEG 4 has been designed with an eye to multimedia systems of the future. It covers the lowest quality audio suitable for voice transmission up to the highest quality for audiophiles and everything in between. It can integrate natural audio, MIDI, speech systems and so on, and allows for interactive content. Much of MPEG 4 is based on Apple's QuickTime format.

MPEG 7 is known as Multimedia Content Description Interface (yes, you have to be good at making up names to work at MPEG). Its aim is to create a standard for describing content to attach to the files themselves so users can search the Web (and their computer systems, of course), for material of interest. The current workplan for MPEG 7 should see it approved before the end of 2001.

When chatting to the MPEG cognoscenti, you may hear the term AAC – Advanced Audio Coding. This is a better method of audio compression which was added to MPEG 2.

Why was MP3 developed?

The various MPEG developments were instigated by the ISO, not to give us fast access to millions of music tracks (they may have had misgivings if they knew then what they know now...), but to save storage space. Yes, in the late 1980s when digital TV was poking its head above the parapet, the ISO saw a need for a standardised method of video compression in order to store the gigabytes of video data which were expected to come on-line.

As video encompasses both video and audio data, it didn't take long for someone to reason that they could use just the audio part of the system to compress audio files. And so MP3 was created although it was a while before the format became widely known and used.

The importance of compression can easily be seen when you consider the size of a 'natural' uncompressed digital audio file. When you record audio digitally, it's stored as a Wave file on the PC, for example. This is a non-compressed format used by virtually all digital audio software. A stereo 'CD quality' recording requires around 10.5Mb of storage space per minute. For a five minute song that's over 50Mb.

Now that's fine if you're putting the music onto a CD, but what if you want to email a friend your latest song or put it on the Web for visitors to download? At the moment most people are still using 56K modems (and some are still plodding along with 28K!). The promise of high speed – and low cost! – Internet access for all is still a long way off. And even when/if it does arrive in the UK and the USA, there's a whole lot of other Net users around the world who won't have access to the technology for many years.

All of which demonstrates the need for fast Internet access or small file sizes. And smaller file sizes are far easier to achieve. With a 56K modem, a four-minute song in Wave format would take around two hours to download. Even with ISDN transfer rates of 128kbps you're looking at 45 minutes. It's only when you reach the transfer capabilities of cable, around 1.5Mbps, that you're looking at a more reasonable four minutes but that's still an hour to download a 60-minute album.

However, if files are compressed, say to a tenth their size, that two-hour download becomes a more reasonable twelve minutes. And most folks are prepared to spend that amount of time downloading a piece of music that they like.

Why MP3 is important for musicians

The MP3 revolution has been gathering momentum since 1997 and came to a head in 1999 and 2000, largely as a result of adverse publicity and high-profile law suits (we don our legal beagle wig in Chapter 3). Illegal aspects of MP3 aside, the ability to compress files to a size to enable transfer via the Internet is a major positive force for music, musicians and music lovers.

The benefits to musicians include the ability to promote their music on the Web. Many artists did this before MP3 but in order to hear the music, visitors often had to download a zipped Wave file or stream a sample of the audio to their computer, neither of which are ideal.

Mac audio

There are two popular audio formats on the Apple Mac – AIFF and SD II. AIFF stands for Audio Interchange File Format and many PC programs support it, too. SD II is named after Digidesign's Sound Designer II software which created it.

On stream

Streaming is the process of transferring data to your computer and playing as it is being received without having to wait until the whole file downloads. There's more about streaming in Chapter 4.

A&R

A&R stands for Artists and Repertoire. These are the guys and gals (but mainly guys) whose job is to spot the next Big Name act and sign them up for a record deal. The more cynical (or perhaps worldy-wise) members of the music community suggest A&R stands for something altogether less polite...

MP3 allows anyone who has recorded a piece of music to convert it into an MP3 file and upload it to the Web. This is such an easy – and cheap! – method of promotion that artists and bands who struggled trying to interest A&R men in their music have been turning to the Web in droves.

Of course, with the whole world and his granny making music and throwing it up on the Web, there's even more dross out there than there was before. However, there are Web sites which promote MP3 music and which aim to filter out the rubbish for you (hmm, sounds a bit like A&R work...). We look at these in Chapter 4.

The advent of MP3 has also made it easy to sell music from a Web site. Artists can put up a sample of their work and then charge a small fee for visitors to download full songs. This can work in several ways. There may be, say, a 30 or 50 second clip of a song, long enough so you know if you want to buy the whole thing. You may be able to hear the song in very low quality audio and if you like it you can buy the high quality version. Or you may get a song or two completely free as an encouragement to buy others.

Consumer benefits of MP3

The cost of songs varies from site to site and artist to artist, but the benefit to the customer is usually a saving in price compared to buying a CD. As there is no physical object – ie. the CD, case, inlay and so on – the 'manufacturing' costs are virtually nil so the savings could be passed on to the consumer.

In practice consumers tend not to see the savings you might imagine – surprise, surprise – particularly when the artist is backed by a major record label. There is, after all, the considerable cost of promoting the artist and if they are a good seller their profits have to pay for all the records which are flops and this is reckoned to be over 90 percent.

But an even bigger bonus for consumers is the ability to buy individual songs. Hands up if you've ever bought a CD because of one or two songs and hated the rest. Yes, join the club. It will be interesting to see if the ability to buy individual songs continues, particularly where major artists and labels are concerned. No one would then be able to create an album containing so-so filler songs because no one would buy it. The smart money says record companies will resist moves to sell songs individually...

The other consumer benefit is that you get the music you want, when you want it, instantly. You don't have to trail down to your local record store (which may not have whatever you want in stock anyway) and you can get it *now* without having to wait a week for a mail order company to pack it and the post office to deliver it.

You also have access to a far greater amount and variety of music on the Web than even the largest record shop in the world could possibly stock. And that can't be bad!

Interest in MP3 seems to have reawakened our interest in music which can only be of benefit to the music industry as a whole. As more music is becoming available and readily accessible, more people are listening to it which means the market for music is growing, which means more musicians are required to produce music to fill the demand. Or so the theory goes. The music business is as tough as ever and you still need good promotion and a spot of luck to get to the top. Talent helps but, as ever, is hardly essential...

Point to ponder

Have you ever wondered why CDs cost more than cassettes? The music is exactly the same and CDs actually cost less than cassettes to manufacture...

How MP3 works

Welcome to the techy chapter. Actually, we're not going to get terribly techy but if you really don't want to read about the ins and outs of digital audio, you will want to read the MP3 compression section and the sections on VBR and MP3 quality. Then you'll know what to look for when downloading MP3 files and what settings to use when you're creating your own.

Digital audio

MP3 is a compressed audio format but it's still digital audio. To understand what it does we need to know a little about digital audio. But just a little.

In particular, we'll have a quick look at sample rates and resolution because they're mentioned a lot in connection with digital audio. In fact, they are largely responsible for the overall quality of the audio.

Sound is simply a series of vibrations. When you pluck a guitar string you can see it vibrate, and the vibrations pass through the air to your ears which, remarkable instruments that they are, convert the vibrations into messages which they send to your brain which interprets them as 'sound'.

Computers aren't as clever as ears or brains although they're jolly good at sums and crunching numbers. In fact, the only thing computers can understand are numbers. So, to allow them to work with sound we have to convert the sound into numbers.

Sample rate

We do the conversion by measuring or 'sampling' the sound every so-often. This is known, naturally enough, as the sample rate, and the more samples we take the more accurate the digital representation of the sound will be. Figure 2.1 contains a representation of a sine wave. At least we can see it's a sine wave but it contains a lot of steps and if a computer played it, it would sound rather rough and grainy.

In Figure 2.2 we have taken more samples so the steps are much smaller. This is a far better representation of our sine wave and it would sound far better than the previous version. Contrast this with Figure 2.3. We can see it's a sine wave – just! – but there really isn't enough data (that is, not enough samples have been taken) to be sure. This would sound like noise.

Sample rates are measured in kHz and CDs use a sample rate of

More digital audio

If you want to know more about digital audio, may we modestly suggest you look at the *Quick Guide to Digital Audio Recording*, by the same publisher which brings you this fine book.

Sine on

A sine wave is a very pure sound and consists only of one harmonic or frequency from which we get the pitch of the note.

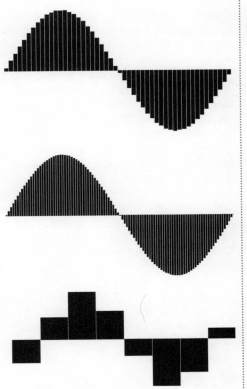

Figure 2.1: A pretty good digital representation of a sine wave...

Figure 2.2 ...but not as good as this one.

Figure 2.3: A sine wave or noise? Our eyes may say sine but our ears would say noise.

44.1kHz which means the sound has been sampled 44,100 times per second. This is by far the most common sample rate but others are used including 48, 32, 22.05 and 11.025kHz. Super high quality systems use 96kHz.

So if we want high quality audio, we use the highest sample rate, right? Right! But there's a trade-off and that is the more samples that are taken, the more storage space they require. And that's about where we came in – trying to cut down the size of audio files.

Sample resolution

The other parameter we're interested in is the sample resolution. This is the fineness of the measuring scale or the range of numbers which are used to store the value of a sample. The sample resolution is measures in bits and the most popular sample resolution is 16 bits.

A bit is a type of number used by computers – you don't want to get any more technical than that, do you? – and 16 bits gives us a

Say when it Hertz

The hertz (abbreviated to Hz) is named after Heinrich Rudolph Hertz and is a measurement representing the number of times an event occurs each second. It is also referred to as CPS or cycles per second. It's common to use kHz (1,000Hz) when talking about sample rates.

numeric range of 65,536. That means that each sample of audio can take a value from 0 through to 65,536. (You can work out the range of numbers so many bits represent by using the old power trick: 2^{16} = 65,536.)

If we used 8 bits, for example, our numeric range would only be 256 (2^8) so the difference between sample measurements would be more coarse and, therefore, the resulting audio less accurate. The current trend in digital audio recording is towards 24-bit recording and some systems are moving up to 32 bits.

So, what does this all mean to the MP3 user? Well, let's get back to kbps which we mentioned in the previous chapter. kbps is the number of thousands of bits used to represent one second of audio. You can calculate the bps by multiplying the sample rate by the sample resolution. CD audio, therefore, is 44,100 x 16 = 705,600bps. To get the kbps, divide by 1024 which makes it around 690kbps. And that's just for mono signals. For stereo recordings we have to double it up to 1378kbps. Although this rate is fine when playing audio from a CD, it's simply too high for Internet transfers.

As you will have gathered, kbps is directly related to file size and quality. We can easily halve the file size by halving the sample resolution or the sample rate but that would also reduce the quality. So what we need is a system that reduces the kbps but maintains the quality.

MP3 compression

Enter MP3. The files are still measured in kbps but the rates are much lower. A typical MP3 file will be just 128kbps although there are other rates as we'll see in a moment.

MP3 compresses audio using a method known as perceptual encoding. This simply means that it uses a psychoacoustic model based on the way the human ear works to identify parts of the signal which can be removed without affecting the sound quality.

For example, our ears find it difficult to place low-pitched sounds in the stereo image. Frequencies below 100Hz don't require as much stereo information as higher frequencies so this can be removed.

The minimum audible threshold is the level below which we are unable to hear a sound. This varies according to frequency because our ears do not respond to all frequencies in the same way. Therefore, frequencies below the threshold can be removed, too. The result of this is, to an extent, subjective because different people have different thresholds which means some people will more easily be able to tell the difference between natural audio and MP3 audio. More of this in a moment.

Lossy vs lossless

As you will have deduced from the comments about removing parts of the audio, MP3 doesn't compress a file in the same way as Zip or Stuffit. With these, when you compress and then expand a file, you always get back exactly what you started with, which is what you need, of course, when compressing word processor documents and spreadsheets. These forms of compression are called lossless.

MP3, however, actually throws away parts of the data and once removed it can never be retrieved. Hence, it is known as a lossy compression system.

The MP3 encoding process uses other psychoacoustic techniques plus standard lossless techniques, too. We don't need to delve into all of them 'cause there's not much we can do to change them but we'll mention one more which is the removal of sounds which are masked by louder sounds. A good example is background noise which might have been picked up by a mic during recording. When the music plays this is totally masked but it's still in the recording so it can be removed with no theoretical loss to the audio.

Age old story

The human range of hearing is generally considered to be between 15Hz and 20kHz. However, we lose sensitivity as we get older – and as we listen to more Heavy Metal and loud Dance music – so it is not unusual for someone in their 20s or early 30s to have an upper range of 16 or 17kHz.

MP3 bit rates

As we mentioned earlier, 128kbps is not the only rate to which MP3 files can be compressed. Depending on the encoding software, you may be able to encode from 8kbps all the way up to 320kbps but, as ever, the higher the bit rate, the larger the file.

Some systems also allow you to select the sample rate, which may vary from 44.1kHz down to 11.025kHz, although you wouldn't use a high sample rate with a low bit rate (say 128kbps with 22.055kHz) because that defeats the object of the exercise. Let's look at some typical compression settings and see what the savings are.

kbps	Sample rate	Compression ratio	Approx. size of 5 min song
1378 (CD audio)	44.1kHz	1:1	52.5Mb
320	44.1kHz	4.4:1	11.9Mb
256	44.1kHz	5.5:1	9.6Mb
192	44.1kHz	7.4:1	7.1Mb
160	44.1kHz	8.8:1	5.9Mb
128	44.1kHz	11:1	4.8Mb
96	44.1kHz	14.7:1	3.6Mb
64	22.05kHz	22.1:1	2.4Mb

kbps	Sample rate	Compression ratio	Approx. size of 5 minute song
56	22.05kHz	25.2:1	2.1Mb
32	11.025kHz	44.1:1	1.2Mb
20	11.025kHz	70.6:1	0.7Mb
8	11.025kHz	176.4:1	0.3Mb

CBR and VBR

To add another level of flexibility (and but a small additional degree of confusion) to the system, there's another consideration with MP3 encoding – whether to use a Constant Bit Rate (CBR) or a Variable Bit Rate (VBR). As its name suggests, CBR uses the same bit rate throughout the entire file. VBR – yes, you guessed – varies the bit rate throughout the file. VBR allows the compression system to use more bits when encoding complex material and fewer bits when the material is simpler. The object is to allow the compression system to retain that little bit extra quality, and VBR should produce better quality audio than CBR at a similar rate.

During encoding VBR can be set to different rates from low to high, perhaps on a scale of 10 to 100 which, of course, affects the file size and quality.

It's impossible to say whether VBR produces larger or smaller files than CBR because that depends upon the material. You'll get the most bang for your buck with files which contain a mix of simple and complex material, perhaps a guitar concerto. But little is likely to be gained by using VBR with modern chart or Dance music which generally has an equal level of complexity throughout.

There are currently two disadvantages with VBR. One is that some portable MP3 players won't play VBR files and some which do are unable to read the song length correctly. This is obviously easy to test for if you have a MP3 player.

The other problem relates to streaming (coming up in Chapter 4). Some streaming systems struggle with VBR because they don't expect the bit rate to vary. Again, this is easy to test and perhaps the situation will get better as streaming technologies improve. The vast majority of MP3 files on the Web are CBR.

MP3 audio quality

So what about the quality of MP3 files? You may have heard some people claim that MP3 is not as good as CD audio, while other people say it is.

The fact is this – it depends! It depends on the listener and how sensitive their ears are. Regardless of how clever the encoding algorithm is, audio material is discarded during the compression process and if you have good and responsive hearing you may well be able to tell the difference.

However, another major consideration which is often ignored is the quality of the playback system. Most MP3s are listened to on computer speakers or on headphones and it would take a very good pair of ears indeed to tell the difference between a CD and a high quality MP3 file under those conditions.

128kbps and 44.1kHz is the 'standard' used on the Internet, and when folks talk about quality and MP3 files, this is usually the rate they're talking about. You may also see 64kbps files on the Internet, and some people say this is like FM radio... But see the next section for more about MP3 quality.

Unless you want to play MP3s through your hi fi, you probably don't need to worry too much about the quality. Test a few rates for yourself and see what sounds acceptable. You may well think 64kbps sounds just fine and if it's okay for you, that's okay with everyone else. However, if you are putting MP3s on the Net, do give people the option of downloading 128kbps files at the least. Many people now use 160kbps just to offer a little more quality.

Once you drop below 64kbps you will easily be able to hear the difference, and rates lower than this are usually only used to give people a flavour of the music or for voice recordings. Because the voice has a far smaller range and is much less complex than music, lower rates can be used while maintaining the legibility of the sound. You may even be able to get as low as 8kbps which would enable you to store 16 times as much material as the 128kbps rate.

In case you're wondering why anyone would want umpteen hours of voice recordings – talking books. These are quite a cult thing in the US of A and people listen to them while stuck in traffic jams on their way to work and while roller skating along the boulevards where the beautiful people hang out.

Other MP3 compression systems

We mentioned the Fraunhofer compression system in the previous chapter but this uses a patented technology which costs a fair few dollars (or Deutschemarks) to license. Software developers who want to include Fraunhofer encoding have to pay a license fee and so must charge for their software. So it's not surprising to learn that there are alternatives to the Fraunhofer encoder, many of which are freely available on the Web.

Saving MP3s

When creating MP3s for their own use many people use 256kbps. It's a very high quality and still offers good compression over Wave files so lots more will fit onto a hard disk or CD. There's more about creating your own MP3s in Chapter 8.

Heavy codecs

Technically, some encoders found on the Web may not be strictly legal. Although the Fraunhofer algorithms were patented, the reference source code was made available on the Web and freely available to anyone who fancied a spot of programming. But then Fraunhofer began to get heavy about people distributing encoders based on the code and forced the algorithms to be removed, but most of the software which used it is still available.

The technology we're talking about is technically called a codec which is short for **co**mpressor/**dec**ompressor. It's not a stand-alone piece of software as such but an algorithm for the encoding and decoding process which can be incorporated into other pieces of software.

Apart from Fraunhofer, the most popular codecs are BladeEnc, Xing and LAME, but there are others including MP3Enc by Opticom, and both MPecker (currently going through a name change to MPegger – what a good idea!) and N2MP3 for the Apple Mac. There are, therefore, dozens of software programs which incorporate various MP3 codecs and we look at some later in the book.

Codec Web sites

BladeEnc: http://bladeenc.mp3.no

LAME: www.sulaco.org

Xing: www.xingtech.com

MP3Enc: www.opticom.de

MPecker: www.anime.net/~go/mpecker.html

MPegger: www.proteron.com/mpegger

N2MP3: www.n2mp3.com

For more information about the quality of MP3 encoders, browse an article on the Web at:

http://arstechnica.com/wankerdesk/1q00/mp3/mp3-1.html

The author ran exhaustive tests using Fraunhofer, LAME, BladeEnc and Xing and reports on his findings. Perhaps it's not surprising that the Fraunhofer codec came top by quite an easy margin, particularly at 128kbps but also at higher rates.

Other digital audio compression formats

Although this is a book about MP3, we wouldn't be giving you the full picture if we didn't mention some alternatives. Although MP3 is very popular with users, it's not so popular with the record companies, so software developers have created other formats which aim to address the concerns of the music industry – namely the ease with which compressed audio files can be copied. We'll mention just a few alternatives.

Microsoft WMA *www.microsoft.com/windows/windowsmedia/en/ download/default.asp*
Windows Media Audio has got to be one of the front runners as the format for protected music distribution. New versions of Windows such as Windows Me (Millennium Edition) come with the Windows Media Player and it's also freely available on the Web. WMA supports copying restrictions and embedded copyright information. It also offers high quality audio and video with good compression ratios. Most MP3 players support WMA.

'Concerned' of Mansion Towers

....

There's more about the music industry's concerns in the next chapter.

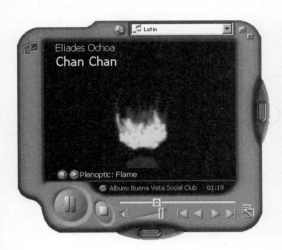

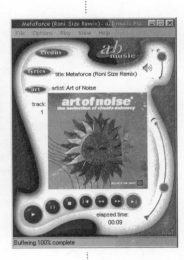

AT&T a2b *www.att.com/campusalliance/a2bmusic.html*
www.a2bmusic.com
When US telecomms giant AT&T saw the amount of interest in digital music, it decided to develop its own format. a2b supports all the features the record companies want to see – encryption, watermarking, copyright protection and royalty tracking. It's a bit short on front-end support but that may change. And it will have to change if consumers are to accept it as an MP3 alternative.

Liquid Audio *www.liquidaudio.com*
This has been around for ages – well, since 1996 which is ages in digital audio terms – and has been used to distribute (ie. sell) music for as long. The format was designed specifically for music distribution and incorporates security and copyright features and facilities which allow the publisher to prevent the file being burned to CD, for example. It has a wide following but it's unlikely to emerge as a major digital music distribution alternative.

Figure 2.4 (left):
Microsoft's all-purpose Media Player, and
Figure 2.5: AT&T's a2b Music Player – secure as Buckingham Palace.

Figure 2.6 (left): Buy music on-line, watch it flow into the Liquid Audio Player.
Figure 2.7: Yamaha's dinky Sound VQ player may be small but it plays beautifully.

Yamaha Sound VQ www.yamaha-xg.com/soundvq
This is a bit of an oddity. It offers excellent audio quality and compression ratios – up to 20:1 – but, as of going to press, it's still in beta and Yamaha doesn't seem to be trying to do anything with it. In its current state it doesn't have much in the way of the restrictions record companies would like so it's not likely to get their vote. However, it's an excellent system that deserves more attention than it's likely to get.

CDs vs MP3s

In Chapter 8 we look at software for converting CD tracks into MP3 files and vice versa but at the moment you might be wondering what the difference is between the two. They're both digital audio formats so if you can put MP3s onto a CD, can you pop it into a normal audio CD player?

Yes you can, but they won't play! The difference lies in the formatting of the data. Essentially an audio CD player sees a CD of MP3s as a CD of computer data – it might as well have program files and word processing documents on it. As you'll know by now, MP3 files have to be decoded by decoding software before they can be played and normal audio CDs players aren't designed to do this. But check Chapter 7 because some CD/MP3 players are starting to appear...

Legal issues

There can be few people who are not aware that laws exist concerned with copying music. However, there are few people – if any! – who understand them all. Not even those you think should know about these things such as the various bodies concerned with looking after music and musicians' rights.

The fact is, music law was already rather involved and the development of the Internet and MP3 just made it a whole lot more complicated. Some of it is still a grey area and it's not unusual for bodies with a vested interest in one area or another to 'interpret' the current state of play to their own advantage.

There is not room in a chapter or even in a book this size to cover all the legal stuff connected with music and MP3s but we will present a brief overview.

Music copyright and wrongs

Music is protected by law and you can't simply copy your favourite CDs and give them to your mates. Apart from being illegal, you are depriving the artists of royalties which they need to live and to write more music. You probably knew that already but it doesn't stop lots of people doing it.

Copyright, as its name suggests, is the 'right to copy' and the copyright holder of a work has the right to say who should be allowed to copy it. Copyright laws vary around the world so make sure you're up to date with the situation in your neck of the woods. In the UK, the author or composer of a work is automatically assigned the copyright when the work is written down or recorded, although you also need to be able to prove that you were in possession of the work before anyone else, which you can do by registering it with a bank or solicitor or by sending the work to yourself in a registered envelope.

Copyright law is complex. The copyright holder has several rights apart from the right to copy the work, including the right to modify it, distribute it and perform it in public. Rights can be sold and licensed and the rights to one thing does not imply the rights to another.

Fair use

Occasionally you will hear someone trot out the term 'fair use'. This relates to a section of copyright law which allows someone to use a 'reasonable' amount of the work without paying a license fee. It is used in book reviews, for example, where the reviewer may quote from the book (a copyrighted property) without payment.

However, it's impossible to apply this to music because there is no definition of what is 'reasonable'. If you want to lift a one second sample from someone's song to use in your own song, this is not considered reasonable and more than one artist who has done so has been embroiled in legal activities

The only safe rule to follow is this: if it belongs to someone else – get permission before you use it.

UK vs USA law

With the proliferation of affordable CD-Rs, many people now create CD compilations of their favourite tracks. Some also copy CDs they already own to play in the car. That would seem reasonable but is it legal?

This is one of the grey areas. In the UK, technically, this is illegal. The question is, when you buy a recording, what do you buy? Do you buy only the right to play and listen to the media that you bought or do you have the right to transfer the music to another type of media and listen to that? Talk to the 'music industry' and they would say the latter although, as far as we are aware, this point has yet to be tested in law.

However, if this was the case, the law would be almost impossible to police so there seems to be a tacit agreement that people can copy music they have bought for their own personal use only.

In the USA the situation is a little clearer because they have a law about it called the Audio Home Recording Act of 1992. This raised a three percent levy on the sale of blank discs and media, plus a two percent surcharge on recording devices such as MiniDiscs and DAT machines. It also sanctions the use of SCMS (Serial Copy Management System) in consumer devices which prevents copies being made from anything but the original material. In other words, it prevents people making a copy of a copy. SCMS was fitted to many consumer DAT machines but it didn't take long before boxes which defeated the SCMS system appeared. SCMS wasn't fitted to professional equipment and was little more than a token gesture.

In return for the levies, users are allowed to copy their own recordings for their own personal use. Which must be good news.

However, there is a lot of opposition to the Act for several reasons. Unlike good ol' British law, it assumes everyone is guilty and there is no opportunity for proving your innocence, and it adopts a teacher mentality – one of you has been naughty so we're going to punish the whole class! (At least that's what teachers were like in the last Millennium!) People who record their own material are being taxed to swell the coffers of the record companies.

It also imposes limits on technology in an attempt to control it

INFO

Countries in Europe have adopted a similar 'blank tape' levy. The UK, showing a most uncharacteristic amount of independence and free-thinking (where were the protagonists' 'incentives'?), did not adopt a similar scheme. But then most things are more expensive in the UK anyway...

(more about this a little latter), and very little of the levy goes to those who need it. Most of the money goes to the record companies – what a surprise! – and most of what they pass on goes to famous artists. Only a small proportion goes to less well-known artists, doubtless assuming that the most popular artists are the ones whose recordings are most likely to be copied.

Are MP3s illegal?

Which brings us to MP3s. Are they illegal? The MP3 file format is certainly not illegal although some files which have been converted into MP3 format may be. Thousands of bands who create their own music have put it on the Web in MP3 format for the express purpose of widespread distribution. This is totally legal. However, you cannot convert songs by your favourite artist into MP3 format and put them up on the Web as this infringes their copyright.

A history of suits

To say that the music industry is unhappy with MP3s is somewhat of an understatement. With an attitude common to many big organisations, first they ignored it, then they tried to force governments to legislate against it; realising that they couldn't do this, they are now trying to control it.

The really dumb thing about it all is that if music companies had had the foresight to recognise the potential of MP3 they could have turned it to their advantage in many ways, not least of all as a new means of music distribution. In fact, this is starting to happen but the behemoth moves with the speed of a sloth and the creativity of a shrike so the easiest option is to sue somebody.

And one of the first cases was against the Diamond Rio, the first hand-held MP3 player to be brought to the mass market (there's more about these devices in Chapter 7). The RIAA claimed that the device should be subject to SCMS restrictions under the Audio Home Recording Act.

The Court of Appeals ruled otherwise and said that under the Doctrine of Fair Use, Rio allowed users to 'space shift' music, a similar principle to that of using a VCR to 'time shift' a video recording. The ruling ought to reinforce users' rights to copy music to another medium in order to listen to it in another place. The court case backfired terribly on the RIAA as it gave an inordinate amount of publicity to Rio and MP3 files. However, Diamond did agree to modify future generations of the Rio player so they would not be able to play files which had encrypted data embedded in them.

INFO

RIAA – Recording Industry Association of America, a heavyweight group representing the US record companies, including major labels, whose job it is to protect their profits.

INFO

....

DMCA – Digital Millennium Copyright Act passed in the USA in 1990. It was intended to provide immunity from law suits to ISPs who unwittingly found themselves hosting or providing links to illegal MP3 files, providing they took steps to remove the offending material when notified. It's impossible for an ISP to monitor every single file or link a user puts up but that didn't stop the IFPI having a go...

MP3.com was also on the receiving end of the RIAA's wrath, but this time the RIAA won. The complaint was about MP3.com's My.MP3.com which allowed users to listen to music from their collection anywhere they had an Internet connection. Before you could listen to a song you had to prove that you owned it by putting the CD in your computer's CD drive. There were ways around this (as there are ways around most restrictions) but the fact that MP3.com actually digitised around 45,000 CDs and held them on their server didn't go down too well and the RIAA won its case. It was a pretty dumb thing of MP3.com to do, really.

Even ISPs (Internet Service Providers) trying to provide helpful and seemingly innocuous services are not safe. Lycos, the search engine, provided a specialist MP3 search engine to help its users find MP3 files. This time the IFPI (International Federation of the Phonographic Industry) took umbrage claiming that the search engine encouraged people to seek out illegal MP3s, an argument that seems comparable to the one which says that selling matches is encouraging people to be arsonists. Anyway, in spite of the DMCA, Lycos backed down.

Napster and friends and enemies

When the cassette tape recorder was developed, the music industry was up in arms, complaining that people would simply copy recordings and record sales would vanish. People did, indeed, copy recordings but it actually lead to an *increase* in music sales. As people became more aware of and discovered more music, they went out and bought their own recordings.

However, giving music to a friend is one thing. With the Internet, one copy of a recording can be distributed to thousands or hundreds of thousands of people extremely quickly and the music industry is, again, concerned over loss of revenue.

Initially, illegal MP3s were posted on temporary Web sites. When the music industry discovered them, they'd make a fuss and the ISP which hosted the site would usually remove it. And the site would spring up again on another server in another place. There are problems, however, if the server is hosted in a country which does not recognise Western copyright laws, but few pirates go to that amount of trouble and at least the Internet copyright police can monitor the situation.

Things changed with the development of Napster. Unlike the Internet which connects individual computers to a central computer, Napster connects individual computers to each other via the Internet. It's specifically designed to allow people to share MP3 files.

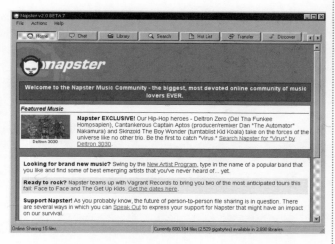

Users can search other people's computers and download MP3 files from them. Obviously, this can be used to transfer illegal MP3s – and it is.

Napster is 'officially' against the swapping of illegal files and as it doesn't hold any of the files on its own server, the legal rights and wrongs of the situation are somewhat blurred. However, it didn't stop the RIAA issuing a law suit against the company. The judge in the case appeared somewhat biased even for America, and ordered the Napster site to be closed. On appeal, however, this decision was overturned, much to everyone's surprise, and Napster lived to swap files another day.

The situation continues as we go to press so check the Napster site (if it's still there) for the latest developments, or log onto some MP3 sites (many are listed in the Appendix) which carry news of happenings in the MP3 world.

But again, the court case backfired on the RIAA. After the amount of publicity Napster received and with the possibility that it might be closed down, it began to attract some 250,000 new users every week!

Now, although Napster positively seems to encourage piracy, it could be used as a means of legitimate music distribution. One suggestion is for users to pay a license fee to access it, much as we pay a radio and TV license fee at the moment. Radio listeners get to hear music and the record companies get paid from the license fee.

If the music industry succeeds in closing Napster, there are many other sites waiting to take over and some offer facilities which the RIAA will certainly not want to see such as anonymous uploading and downloading – check out Freenet. Ouch! The sooner the music industry embraces and works with the technology, the sooner it will

INFO

After the success of
Napster, it was inevitable
that similar software
would appear. Here are
some other sites offering
similar file sharing
services. They were up
there as this book is
being prepared but they
may or may not be there
by the time you log on...
www.napster.com
http://freenet.sourceforge
.net
http://gnutella.wego.com
www.scour.com
www.spinfrenzy.com
www.cutemx.com

find itself back on the playing field. However, the game is changing
as we see in a moment, and the music industry does not like
change.

Does piracy affect music sales?

The music industry, like the software industry, claims it is losing
money through piracy. However, the figures that various bodies
come up with to show how much they are losing is open to
question.

There is a difference between the number of illegal copies which
may be in circulation and the number of people who may have
bought a product if they did not have a pirate copy – which is not to
condone the copying of any product illegally but, for example, if ten
people have a pirate copy of a song, this does not necessarily equate
to the loss of ten sales as some would have us believe. If it were not
possible to acquire pirate material, perhaps ten people would have
bought it, but perhaps only two or three of those ten would have
bought or maybe none.

Surveys have been commissioned by the music industry which
indicate that music sales in the areas surrounding student quarters
(where Napster is most prevalent) have shown a decline. On the
other hand, other surveys found no decrease in sales at all and in
some cases sales had actually risen, due to the increased awareness
and promotion of music created by interest in MP3s. We must
question reports and the motives of those who would restrict our
personal and legal use of material which we have bought and paid
for. So read 'industry' reports with a wary eye.

A contributing factor towards piracy is the high price of CDs.
Even though a UK government commission came to the conclusion
that CDs were too expensive and ought to be reduced (although not
by much), nothing was done to enforce this conclusion and prices
remain as high as ever.

A survey by the Pew Internet Project (www.pewinternet.org)
revealed that users think the price of on-line tracks is too high. No
amount of legislation will prevent piracy – the solution is for
companies to offer more choice and fairer prices so that there is little
need to 'steal' music. Until that happens the record companies will
be fighting an uphill battle which might protect profits in the short
term but which could do irrevocable damage to the industry in the
longer term.

Price cannot justify piracy – if you can't afford a product you
don't clone it – but a sense of 'value' is a major contributing factor
towards it and people obviously don't feel they are getting value for

money. The music industry complained that certain Web sites are 'contributing to copyright infringement' but the high price of CDs must also be a contributing factor.

DRM and SDMI

So, it's in everyone's interest to devise a system which prevents piracy without infringing on the legal rights of those who have bought the music. To that end, the music industry has been looking at systems which restrict or prevent the copying of digital music. The two terms you'll hear in connection with this are DRM (Digital Rights Management) and SDMI (Serial Digital Music initiative).

DRM is about making it possible for companies to distribute digital works such as on-line books and music over the Internet while retaining control over how the work is accessed and copied. The system can also include an accounting system where users have to register so suppliers know exactly who has their products and where they are.

You may not have considered this before, but there are several ways to limit the use of a digital work. It would be encrypted, of course, and require a special reader or player in order to see or hear it. The work could carry with it a limit on the number of times it could be accessed which the player would recognise and after so-many plays, it simply wouldn't, er, play. It's not totally dissimilar to the timed-out protection system used by demo software.

Another option is a pay-per-listen system whereby you buy the right to listen to a work so-many times after which the player will stop playing it, but you can buy more 'listens'.

The SDMI is a collection of around 200 companies whose aim is to create a technology which will protect the playing and distribution of digital music. This is done by encryption and watermarking. The watermarking is very clever because it embeds copyright information into the audio data without, supposedly, altering the character of the audio data in any way.

We'll leave the Hows to the techno bods, but music enthusiasts have expressed concern over the alteration of music data in this way. The SDMI has subjected the audio to tests by a panel of 'golden ears', so-called industry experts, and claimed that they were unable to tell the difference between marked and unmarked audio.

Much of the scepticism stems from the fact that the SDMI refuses to name any of the 'golden ears' so there is really no authority on which to base the claim. While many music authorities agree that inaudible watermarking might be possible with lo fi Internet audio, they wait to be convinced that watermarks can be added to hi

INFO

A recording artist typically gets around three percent of the retail price of a CD.

fidelity audio without any audible trace. We'll be able to judge for ourselves as and when the system comes on-line

Is Big Music Brother watching you?

There's yet another concern from members of privacy groups. Some of the suggestions for the protection of music require the user to supply personal information in order to unlock a playback system. Uniquely identifying information could be used to track anyone who accessed a recording and a database of users who have accessed particular recordings could be made.

Some of this may seem innocuous but you'd be surprised how much personal information about you is already out there and freely available to various organisations and individuals. And once Big Brother has access to it, we're one step nearer to 1984 (if you'll pardon the retrogressive reference). In America in particular, the First Amendment supports the right to free and anonymous thinking and listening.

It's unlikely that such intrusive measures would be incorporated into a SDMI scheme because of the outrage which would be stirred up – but you never know. The aim at the moment seems to be to devise a format which will allow a certain number of copies, maybe three or four, to be made which could be played on SDMI devices but they would not allow a copy of a copy to be made.

SDMI devices would not only play SDMI encrypted music but also unencrypted music such as MP3 files. The object would to be to allow music creators to determine how their music can be played and accessed.

The future of MP3

So does SDMI spell the death knell of MP3? That's a toughie, but the considered answer has to be, not in the short term. There are too many MP3 files out there for them to disappear overnight. Too many people have invested in the software for creating MP3s and in the software and hardware for playing them. They don't want MP3s to disappear and as long as they can continue making MP3s, they're unlikely to do so.

One thing that might hurry the demise of MP3 is if a superior format is produced with higher quality audio and smaller file sizes. But it would still have to offer the portability of MP3 files. People don't like MP3 just because it produces smaller audio files but because it can easily be copied and transferred to other playback systems. Such a development is unlikely so MP3s will doubtless be around for a good while yet.

Now that you've discovered the wonders of MP3s, you want to know where to find them. A good place to start is at some of the dedicated MP3 sites. We'll look at a few here to get you started and there's a longer list in the Appendix.

But first, you need to know how get the file from the Web site onto your hard disk.

How to download an MP3 file

Downloading an MP3 is essentially the same as downloading any file so if you've transferred software from the Web to your computer before you'll be an old hand at it.

Most MP3 sites have text or a button or two alongside the name of a song file. One is usually for streaming (coming up) and the other for downloading.

Many sites pop up helpful context-sensitive descriptions of the buttons when you rest the mouse pointer on them which tell you exactly what they do. The Vitaminic site is one such example and Figure 4.1 clearly shows that this button will stream a file while Figure 4.2 shows that the next button will download it, and it tells you how big it is.

4

MP3s – where to find them, how to get them

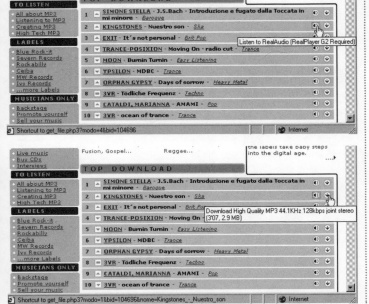

Figure 4.1: Vitaminic's helpful pop up descriptions tell you that this button will stream the audio...

Figure 4.2: ...while this one will download it, and it tells you how big it is.

Figure 4.3: The Download dialogue box tells you the name of the file you are about to save.

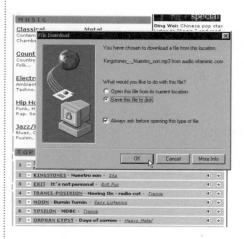

Clicking on the download button should start the download, Figure 4.3, unless you're at a site which requires copious amounts of personal information before it lets you download a file – and some do, you know. The exact response you get from such a button may also depend upon your browser, but it should eventually offer to save the file to your hard disk. It will supply the name of the file and let you navigate to the directory in which you want to save it.

It's often easier to right-click on the button or link and select Save Target As (again, this facility may depend upon your browser), Figure 4.4, from the pop-up menu, which should then take you to the Download dialogue in Figure 4.3.

However, do check that this link is a direct link to the file and

Figure 4.4: Right-clicking on a download link will allow you to save the file to disk.

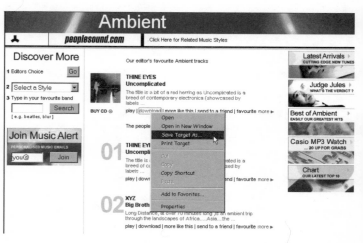

not a link to another page where you may have to enter additional personal information, otherwise you'll be saving a Web page and not a file. You can usually tell by looking in the Status Bar at the bottom of the browser when you rest the mouse pointer on the button or link. In Figure 4.2 you can see that the Status Bar at the bottom of the browser window shows the name of the file. If it linked to another page it would probably show the name of the page, maybe saying something like 'Shortcut to...'

And that's it! You can then go and have a cup of coffee or read War and Peace while the file downloads. Check the Interrupted Downloads section a little later to see how to increase your peace of mind during downloading.

Streaming

One of the problems with large files is that you have to download the entire file in order to listen to it and you may discover you don't like it. Some sites used to get around this by offering smaller sample files for downloading but most sites now use streaming technology.

Streaming is a neat idea. Essentially, it starts playing a file as soon as some of it has been received so you don't have to wait until all of it has been downloaded. It requires little user intervention; all the mechanics are handled by the software.

Most sites use RealAudio for streaming although some use MP3 streaming and some, like BeSonic, give you the choice of both. To receive RealAudio files, you need a copy of RealPlayer. Most MP3 sites have a link to this and you can get it direct from the RealAudio Web site.

In order to work well, streaming technology needs the data to be received more quickly than it needs to be played so you need a fast connection. If you recall, most MP3 files have a bit rate of 128kbps so if you try to stream a 128kbps file you need a 128kbps connection. Actually, you need a faster connection because some of the capacity is used for communications overheads. If you have a 56K modem, for example, you'll know that you rarely get a connection faster than 48K, and that's doing well.

If a connection cannot deliver the stream as quickly as it is being played, the player will stop playback until it receives more data and it will probably tell you that it is buffering the data. As most folks are still using 56K modems or even slower ones, most sites use low quality files for streaming. Some may even offer a choice of lo fi or hi fi streaming.

But whether or not playback stutters is not of major importance here. The important thing is that you can quickly tell if you like a

TIP

If you don't have a Status Bar at the bottom of Internet Explorer, make sure the Status Bar entry in the View menu is checked.

INFO

RealAudio is another compressed audio format, usually with a .ram extension, and not as high quality as MP3. You can get more info from: http://realguide.com www.real.com

piece of music enough to download it all. And if you do, you click on the download link. For more information about streaming audio surf to:

http://members.aol.com/mbmband/html/streaming.html

There is lots of streaming software at:

www.hitsquad.com/smm/cat/STREAMING_AUDIO_MEDIA

It's worth mentioning that you can stream video as well as audio, and some sites include 'performance' videos either for streaming or downloading. If you think audio files are big, video files are massive and streaming a video of any size is not a realistic option with a 56K connection.

Quick start – MP3 music sites

You're keen to begin so here are a few sites with thousands of MP3 files you can start investigating.

peoplesound.com (www.peoplesound.com)
One of the major and most highly-promoted MP3 sites featuring thousands of tracks by unsigned artists, mostly British. Tracks are neatly divided into genres covering everything from rock to indie and folk to classical. You can type in the name of your favourite band and the search will produce a lists of songs and artists in a similar style – 'if you like that, you'll like this'. Very neat. It has Top 20 selections, an Editor's Choice, competitions, features and loads more.

BeSonic www.besonic.com
Another top site with thousands of downloads and dozens of music categories. There's usually information about the artist which helps you find out where they're coming from, and when you select a band, you get a list of other artists who produce music in a similar style. The site also contains lots of MP3 information.

Vitaminic www.vitaminic.co.uk
Yet another large site with thousands of files arranged by genre. The Top 10 is on the front page so you can quickly see what's new, and there are lots of articles and features. The site is very easy to navigate and the files are easy to download. A must to bookmark.

MP3.com www.mp3.com
The granddaddy of MP3 sites containing thousands of files listed by category on the front page. There's artist information, info about

---

TIP

....

Some sites take you through several download pages and make you enter an email address before you can access the download area. The concern is that you will be bombarded with spam and your email address sold, regardless of 'privacy promises' on the site. So remember that the address you enter does not have to be a genuine one...

MP3 hardware and software, gear lists, plus a whole range of MP3 stuff. And, having been on the receiving end of the RIAA's ire (see Chapter 3), there are up-to-date links to news items of interest to the MP3 community.

MP3 Direct Download www.mp3dd.net

Well over 100,000 files, Top 50 downloads, lots of general MP3 info, charts by Billboard, the UK Top 40 and MTV. There are lots of links to other MP3 sites, videos, full albums, and an MP3 archive. On the downside, music isn't listed by genre making it difficult to browse unless you know what you're looking for. It throws up dozens of pop-up windows which is annoying in the extreme and many of the MP3s are linked to from external sites. In short, it's a pain use but it's included here because of the sheer number of files it offers access to.

Figure 4.5(left):
peoplesound.com has thousands of files, neatly categorised.

Figure 4.6 (right):
Vitaminic has lots of files in lots of categories and they're very easy to download.

Figure 4.7; Thousands of downloads on MP3 Direct Download but those pop-ups are annoying as hell.

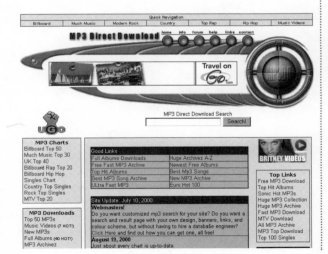

Figure 4.8: Hundreds of free and to-pay-for classical music MP3 downloads from eClassical.

MusicBlitz *www.musicblitz.com*
Up-to-date site with lots of downloads from Big Name artists and underground acts. Music is divided into genres all relatively modern – no classics here but there is Jazz, Blues, Reggae and Rock. There are features, top downloads and a help section. Nice.

eClassical *www.eclassical.com*
As its name suggests, this is devoted to classical music. It contains hundreds of files, some are free but some cost a few pennies.

Jazz Promo *www.jazzpromo.com*
Yes, a Jazz site with lots of info, features, interviews and, as of writing, over ten hours of free MP3 files.

audible.com *www.audible.com*
A commercial site offering downloadable audio books. There are all sorts of categories covering fiction, non-fiction, business, science, foreign languages, comedy. history, mystery and so on, and there are free samples, too.

Comedy Circus *www.comedycircus.com*
Yes, you can listen to jokes on the Internet. There are lots of clips from classic comedians such as Eddie Izzard, Jo Brand, Ben Elton and Barry Cryer, and you can buy the albums, too.

Internet record labels

On your travels through cyberspace in search of MP3 files you may discover some Internet record labels. Many are essentially similar to traditional record labels but aim to promote artists and sell their music via the Internet. This, theoretically, should be more cost-effective than traditional methods of artist promotion, although some Internet labels use traditional methods of promotion, too.

Figure 4.9 Fancy a laugh? Book a seat at the Comedy Circus.

As there are no CDs to manufacture, the cost of music distribution is negligible which ought to result in cheaper music for the consumer yet larger profits for the company. Artists generally receive a larger proportion of the sale price than they would with a traditional record company, although that needs to be balanced with the expected number of sales which may – or may not – be greater using traditional methods of promotion.

The major record labels have been slow to take advantage of the Internet for music distribution (see Chapter 3) but are now starting to get their act together and allowing their music to be distributed on the Net.

Most Internet record labels major on independent and hitherto unsigned artists. Although most Internet record labels offer free samples for downloading, remember that the thrust of their business is to sell music.

10X Records www.10xrecords.com
A definite Internet-only record label which says it's not limited to any particular music type.

amp3.com www.amp3.com
A clear site with music news and features plus free MP3s. It allows artists to create their own Web site and share in profits.

Atomic Pop www.atomicpop.com
As it says, pop music with artist info, free downloads and the ability to buy.

Big Heavy World www.bigheavyworld.com
Big Heavy World. Big dark Web site. Artist info, catalogue, pics and MP3s.

Confidential Records www.cadmanlane.fsnet.co.uk
An Internet record label offshoot of a recording studio. Audition the CDs and buy them if you like them.

Figure 4.10: Artists can create their own site at amp3.com.

EMusic www.emusic.com

A big site which some may not consider a 'traditional' Internet record label. It distributes music for over 600 labels, 6,700 artists and it has over 125,000 MP3s. You can pay per download or get access to unlimited downloads for a very modest monthly fee. Songs are organised by style and the site is easy to navigate.

Hanging Stone www.hangingstone.co.uk

Attractive site annoyingly powered by Flash. Artist info and free downloads. It claims to be the first on-line record company that disables the ability to burn tracks to CD.

J. Bird Records www.j-birdrecords.com

Browse by genre, listen to a track, buy the CD. Also contains news and info on new artists and releases.

Kaleidospace www.kspace.com

A resource for independent artists of all kinds, not just musicians but it features lots of music in a broad range of categories including a novelty section containing sub-categories such as Dixieland Death Rock, Ironic Music Comedy and Bizarre Revelations. Interesting.

Spin Records www.spinrecords.com

A large site with music divided into categories. There are slideshows, information on new artists, spin radio and webcast archives (see the next chapter for more about webcasting), and more.

Utopian Trance www.utopiantrance.co.uk

'Think of it as a sort of on-line record company, similar to mp3.com but without all the eleven-year olds using Dance eJay,' it says.

MP3 search engines

Dedicated MP3 sites may contain hundreds or thousands of files. Most sites organise them into categories or genres, and many have a search engine to make it easy to find specific songs or artists. Naturally, search engines tend to concentrate on the contents of their own site so if you can't find what you're looking for you need to look a little further afield.

Open your favourite search engine, perhaps Google (www.google.com), enter 'MP3' and stand well back. MP3 Web sites have been propagating like bunnies and you will get thousands, probably hundreds of thousands of hits. It's not practicable to check all the sites; you need a more accurate way to find specific material. You need a specialist MP3 search engine.

MP3 search engines work exactly like ordinary search engines but, obviously, only look for MP3 files. You won't be surprised to learn that there are lots of them, so many, in fact, that we need a search engine to search for the best MP3 search engines...

Surf over to MP3 Now (www.mp3now.com). This tracks a Top 30 list of the best MP3 search engines as voted for by its visitors. This may have changed by the time you read this but as of writing, the Numero Uno is Palavista (www.palavista.com), Figure 4.11, which is a metacrawler. Most search engines have their own database of sites which they have catalogued and that's what you search. A metacrawler sends your query to several search engines at the same time and then sorts and tabulates the results. Neat, eh?

Audio Valley (www.audiovalley.com) also has a list of its favourite MP3 search engines covering HTTP and FTP sites (more about these in a moment). It also includes a few hints and tips about MP3 and downloading music.

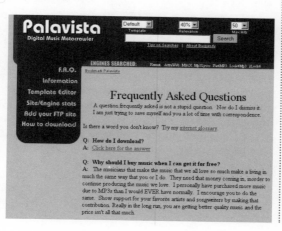

Figure 4.11: Palavista, an MP3 search engine highly rated by MP3 searchers...

The Internet and the Web

The Internet is the vast conglomeration of interlinked computers that we access when we log on and 'surf the Net'. Technically, the Web is a method of accessing the Internet using graphic-based browsers such as Internet Explorer and Netscape. In practice most people use the terms 'Internet' and 'Web' interchangeably – and we do, too – but strictly speaking the Web is a subset of the Internet.

Other sites to look at include MP3 Board (www.mp3board.com), which has an HTTP and a FTP search engine, and can perform a Gnutella search (Gnutella allows MP3 file sharing like Napster).

But MP3 Now can go one better than these. It has devised its own metacrawler engine which searches all the MP3 search engines in its Top 30! There's a link to it from the site and you'll find it at www.findsongs.com.

HTTP and FTP

The Internet started to achieve mass popularity when it became easy to use, which was with the development of the World Wide Web and user-friendly browsers. The Web uses hyperlinks to jump from one site to another and to do this it uses a system called HTTP or Hypertext Transfer Protocol. That's why most Web addresses begin with http://

Before the Web, people accessed files on the Internet using an interface more like DOS (anyone remember that?) which required typing in strings of commands. Very unfriendly. This system was called FTP (File Transfer Protocol) and FTP functionality is built in to many browsers so you can access files via FTP through a graphic interface. FTP pages look more like the display you get with Windows Explorer than the graphic displays we're used to with Internet Explorer. You can tell if you're at an FTP site because the address begins with ftp://

What's the benefit of FTP? Well, HTTP wasn't really designed for transferring large files, and although it can handle bitmap graphics and text well enough, sometimes it struggles with large downloads, as you may have noticed. Many sites which contain lots of files – these can be program files, graphics or MP3 files – use FTP so if you come across a good MP3 FTP site you might find it better to transfer files via FTP than HTTP.

Browsers don't always offer full FTP support and it's often easier to use a dedicated FTP program. With such programs you can usually transfer files simply by dragging them from the host server window and dropping them into your window so it's not terribly difficult to use although sometimes setting up can be a little involved.

There are several FTP programs available including CuteFTP, Figure 4.12, (available from www.cuteftp.com) for the PC, and Fetch (available from www.dartmouth.edu.pages/softdev) for the Apple Mac. CuteFTP has a built-in search feature for finding MP3 files.

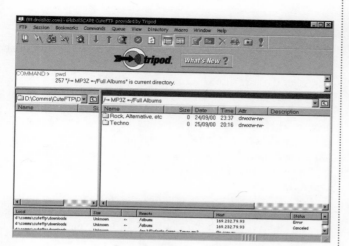

Figure 4.12: CuteFTP
makes FTP as relatively
easy as FTP can be.

FTP tips

There is a ton of information about FTP on the Web. Try these:

http://webreference.com/roadmap/map13.html
http://coba.shsu.edu/help/ftp/faq.html
www.faqs.org/faqs/ftp-list/
www.sonoma.edu/IT/FAQ/Fetch/fetch.htm

Ratio sites

One advantage of using an FTP site is that FTP is rather techy for the majority of Internet users so the sites should not be very busy which means you ought to be able to download files faster.

There is one disadvantage with some FTP sites, however, and that is that many are ratio sites. This means that you must upload so-many files before you can download any. Some ratios are 1:1 but others are more generous with ratios of 1:4. However, this does mean you have to spend time uploading a file or two before you can download some which may negate the speed benefits of FTP.

But not all FTP sites are ratio sites and the benefits of a good site outweigh the disadvantages. Ratio sites are generally not a good idea unless you have a connection faster then 56K.

Interrupted downloads

Have you ever tried to download a large file only to find that the server closes the connection or the line drops when you're 90 percent of the way through! Annoying isn't it?

You can often resume interrupted downloads with FTP and you may find this option in FTP software. If you're using a browser, you need a pieces of software such as Go!Zilla (www.gozilla.com), or Get Right (www.getright.com). These allow you to resume an interrupted download. If you got part of a file, they will resume at that point so you don't have to download from the start all over again. Good, eh?

Not all sites support resumed transfers, and Go!Zilla, for example, will tell you if they do when downloading a file, but many sites do and this is certainly a facility worth having.

These programs can do all sorts of other clever stuff, too, such as scheduling downloads for a certain time and disconnecting and shutting down the computer afterwards. They have search facilities and can check that you have the latest version of software you want to download. If you're downloading large files you need one of these.

Fixing MP3 files

Most sites which distribute MP3s have got the hang of it and there are rarely any problems other than interrupted downloads. However, occasionally problems can occur and a file may not be received correctly or it may not play. This can happen if the server supplying the MP3 file is not configured correctly, a process called 'cooking'.

Your best option is to surf off to another site but if you really want the file, there is a program you can use to try to fix it. It's called Uncook95 and you can get it from: http://free-music.com/uncook95.htm. The site explains what 'cooking' is and what the program does – we're not going to get into the technicalities here.

The site also contains another utility called Unphuck (how imaginative), which also has a stab at repairing MP3s and removing ID3 tags (there's more about these in Chapter 6) which can prevent playback in certain MP3 players. Again, the site has all the details.

5

I n the previous chapter we mentioned streaming. This essentially transmits music (or other sounds) to your computer in real time. Sounds rather like what radio does...

Internet radio

And it didn't take long for some enterprising people to develop the idea of Internet radio. You 'tune in' to a Web site or channel which simply streams music to you. Wow! Lo fi music through the cumbersome media of a PC. What's the point?

There are several points. First of all, traditional radio is one-way communication. With Internet radio, the listener has more control over the program content and can skip a song, for example, if they don't like it.

There are several thousand Internet radio channels and the numbers are increasing all the time. They offer masses of variety, allowing stations to cater for many minority interests. For example, you don't just get a classical music channel, you get a channel devoted to a specific composer. There are channels which play one particular type of music such as Ambient or Trance. And if you've just split up with a partner, there are channels which specialise in 'breakup' songs.

Internet radio is not limited to music – there are talk shows, spoken word channels, religion, sport, news, finance, political comment, history... you name it, there's probably an Internet radio channel covering it. Many terrestrial radio channels also broadcast on the Internet. This allows them to reach listeners who are not within their transmitter range and it means you can listen to your favourite radio programs wherever you are in the world – providing you have an Internet connection.

Have you ever heard a song on the radio and the dumb DJ didn't bother to tell you what it was? Most (but not all) Internet radio stations clearly show the artist and title of the song which is currently playing.

Many radio sites have a My Radio Station facility which allows you to customise the content you receive. You can choose from a list of song types and say how often you want to hear them and the site will assemble a customised playlist when you log on. You can mix and match a whole range of styles.

Finally, some sites broadcast video, too, so you can listen to songs and watch the video.

Internet radio and webcasting

Song skipping

'Ah! Ha!' cries the attentive reader. 'If music is being streamed in real-time, how can you skip a song?' If the material is being generated in real-time, you can't, but most sites which play music create a program or playlist of songs assembled ahead of time. This is what is streamed when you tune in, making it easy to skip a song. Also, some sites which let you create your own Radio Station – coming up – put together a playlist at the time you tune in, again making it easy to skip a song in the list. Many stations keep archives of earlier broadcasts which you can also access – and skip.

INFO
....
20kbps is the highest rate
normally recommended
for users with a 28.8K
modem.

Internet radio quality

This brings us back to the major limitation of streaming – download speed. If you just want to listen to a piece of a song to see if you like it enough to download, you can tolerate a few hiccups. However, trying to listen to continuous broadcast which constantly stops and start is very annoying. Therefore, your Internet connection speed determines the quality of the audio you can receive.

Fortunately, most sites offer low-bandwidth broadcasts which could be from 16 to 32kbps, suitable for users with 56K modems. There may also be higher rate of 56kbps for those with faster connections.

Because of the bandwidth consideration, most stations broadcast in mono, although a few broadcast in stereo, too, or have both mono and stereo options. It's relatively pointless trying to listen to a stereo broadcast unless you have a connection faster than 56K.

Other factors affect the reception, too, such as how busy the server is. If it's a popular station and you log on at peak time, the server may struggle to provide you with a steady stream of data. If you do other tasks on your PC, surf to other sites and download files, this could cause glitches, too.

How to receive Internet radio

It's very easy to receive Internet radio. The main requirement is software which supports streaming data. Different sites and stations use different software but it's all readily and freely available. Most sites use the RealPlayer, many use Windows Media Player, some are quite happy with an MP3 player such as WinAmp (more of which in Chapter 6), and some pop-up a mini browser window and play through that. Mac users can use QuickTime. You then log on to the station's Web site, click on a station and that's it!

Figure 5.1: Aladdin's MacTuner – Internet radio for Mac users.

Figure 5.2: Windows Media Player offers quick access to hundreds of Internet radio stations.

There are dedicated pieces of software for listening to Internet radio such as vTuner (www.vtuner.com), Earth Tuner (www.earthtuner.com), and MacTuner, Figure 5.1, for the Mac (www.aladdinsys.com), but unless you really become a devotee, you'll find that your Web browser, RealPlayer, Windows Media Player and an MP3 player are all you need.

Windows Media Player, Figure 5.2, has a Radio Tuner tab and clicking on it brings up a list of featured radio stations. To the right is a Station Finder where you can search for stations by format, language, location and by the type of music it plays. You can also create your own preset lists of favourite stations.

RealPlayer, Figure 5.3, has several built-in buttons for selecting radio stations which range from sport, news and technology to business, comedy and, of course, music. It lists sites with music videos, too. You can customise the list and there's a Radio Tuner feature which searches the Web for stations by various criteria including music type.

Figure 5.3: RealPlayer's Radio Tuner lets you search the Web for Internet radio stations.

Finding Internet radio stations

There are so many Internet radio stations that finding them is not a problem. Type 'Internet radio' into a search engine and you'll get thousands of hits. Plus, media players such as RealPlayer and Windows Media Player have built-in station search facilities. However, if you want to explore some of the other sites on the Web, here are a few to get you started.

Antenna Radio www.antennaradio.com
A classy site, Figure 5.4, broadcasting ten or so programs covering an eclectic range of styles encompassing classics, jazz, punk, Japanese pop, experimental, contemporary, country and psychedelic rock. It also has lots of links to other selected radio sites.

Figure 5.4: Antenna Radio broadcasts several programs covering an eclectic range of music.

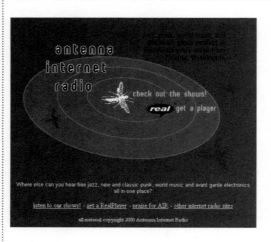

Billboard Radio www.billboardradio.com
Lots of music and music information from this industry-standard newspaper and Web site. It lists the Top 100 and currently features a weekly Chart Countdown broadcasting at 28K, 56K and 100K, and it uses Windows Media Player.

In Perpetual Motion www.gothicindustrial.com
Gothic – Industrial – Electronic – Internet – Radio. It says. Very well presented, Figure 5.5, with a large archive of past shows. It can use RealPlayer or an integrated browser player which shows the playlist. Quality site.

Internet Radio Index www.internetradioindex.com
A tasteful, understated site with lots of links to lots of stations grouped by country. An essential visit.

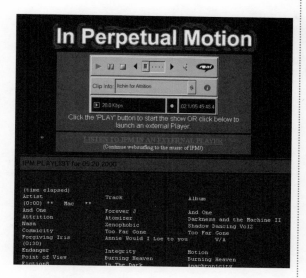

Figure 5.5: In Perpetual Motion keep Gothic and Industrial music on the move.

K-Tel Radio www.ktel.com/radio.html
King of the Kompilations, K-Tel's radio station, Figure 5.6 has exactly the sort of music you'd expect, broadcasting at 28K and 56K.

Figure 5.6: All you'd expect from the K-Tel record label.

Kids Internet Radio www.kir.org
Primarily for the kiddies and primarily for the Americans but do give it a shot – Listen With Mother will never be the same.

Radio Paradise www.radioparadise.com
A veritable paradise for some – 'the Web's intelligent rock alternative' – with broadcasts in both mono and stereo.

Internet radio lists

Needless to say, there are also many sites containing radio lists and links to radio sites.

Google Web Directory http://directory.google.com/Top/Arts/Radio/Internet
A large list of hundreds of radio sites covering categories such as comedy, music, news, regional, sports and talk radio.

Internet Radio List www.internetradiolist.com
A large list of stations in lots of categories with regular information about featured stations, a list of new stations and lots of Internet-related links, Figure 5.7.

Figure 5.7: There are links, stations and lists at Internet Radio List.

Kerbango www.kerbango.com
A smart site with a vast range of station categories, Cool Stream suggestions, quick search as well as advanced search features, and the ability to limit searches to stations with the bandwidth which your system can manage.

Radio Tower www.radiotower.com
Lists of over 1,300 stations with Stations, Country and Category search parameters. It pops up a small browser to play a selected station but can use RealPlayer and Windows Media Player, too.

Sonicnet http://radio.sonicnet.com
Lots of stations, lots of categories and a really neat feature to let you create your own customised radio station by selecting music categories you'd like to hear, Figure 5.8. It pops up its own browser

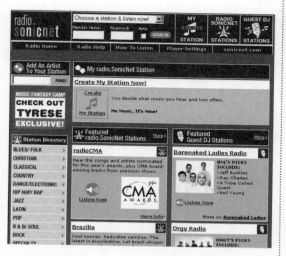

player and you can further fine-tune your list when it plays a song buy saying whether you'd like to hear more or less of the artist. Neat.

Shoutcast Showcase www.shoutcast.com
Named after the software which lets anyone create their own Internet radio station – coming up in a mo – this features lots of stations and lets you search by music category and connection speed.

Spinner www.spinner.com
'The most variety you'll find anywhere,' it says and it may just be true. It requires its own player which is free to download and boasts over 140 music channels and 350,000 songs.

Virtual Reference Site – Audio www.virtualfreesites.com/reference. audio.html
Lots of links to radio sites and to sites containing information of interest to Internet radio users.

Web-Radio www.web-radio.com
Over 4,200 stations, searchable in many ways. It lists the stations, their speed and the player they use.

Internet Radio restrictions

It will come as no surprise to learn that the powers that be tend to be very wary of Internet radio. They reason that if a listener can choose the artists or even the songs they want to hear whenever they want, they would not go out and buy the CDs. And if music is being played and heard, the copyright holders want some money.

Therefore, there are restrictions on what can be played and when, conditions that were devised by the RIAA. There's quite a list of them and we copy here extracts from just a few from the RIAA Web site:

1 Pay royalties.
2 A webcaster may not play in any three-hour period (1) more than three songs from a particular album, including no more than two consecutively, or (2) four songs by a particular artist or from a boxed set, including no more than three consecutively.
3 Prior announcements are not permitted. DJ 'teaser' announcements using artists' names are permitted, but only those that do not specify the time a song will be played.
4 Archived programs – those that are posted on a web site for listeners to hear repeatedly on-demand – may not be less than five hours in duration. Those that are five hours or more may reside on a web site for no more than a total of two weeks. Merely changing one or two songs does not meet this condition.
5 Looped or continuous programs – those that are performed continuously, automatically starting over when finished – may not be less than three hours in duration. Again, merely changing one or two songs does not meet this condition.
6 Programs under one hour in duration that are performed at scheduled times may be performed only three times in a two-week period, four times if one hour or more in duration.
7 A webcaster must identify the sound recording, the album and the featured artist if receivers of the service are capable of displaying this information.
8 A webcaster may not perform a sound recording in a way that falsely suggests a connection between the copyright owner or recording artist and a particular product or service.
9 A webcaster must disable copying by a transmission recipient if in possession of the technology to do so, and must also take care not to induce or encourage copying by transmission recipients.
10 Requirement to accommodate technical protection measures. A webcaster must accommodate the transmission of

measures widely used by sound recording copyright owners to identify or protect copyrighted works if it is technically feasible to transmit them without imposing substantial burdens on the transmitting entity.

11 A webcaster must co-operate with copyright owners to prevent recipients from using devices that scan transmissions for particular recordings or artists.

INFO

You can read the full list of webcasting conditions at the licensing section of the RIAA's site: www.riaa.com.

You can see from the above that the authorities take the 'threat' of Internet radio broadcasting very seriously. Of particular concern is the thought that listeners might download broadcast material. Most audio players, however, will not allow this, and if you scan your hard disk after a broadcast you'll find that the audio data is not there. If broadcast music could be downloaded that would constitute music distribution, not music broadcasting, which is a different license altogether and not one which all record companies are currently prepared to offer.

There is software, however, which can direct streamed audio to disk and you can grab a free copy of Voquette Media Manager from www.voquette.com. Get it now before they ban it! There's more about this in the next chapter. But be aware that currently, streamed data may be very low quality.

Webcasting

The intrepid reader may now be wondering if it's possible for anyone to set up an Internet radio station. The simple answer is yes, and the most popular piece of software for doing this is called Shoutcast, available from www.shoutcast.com. Shoutcast uses MP3 and it can deliver live broadcasts as well as audio-on-demand for archived broadcasts.

Broadcasting is rather more involved than simply receiving stations and beyond the scope of this book, but the site explains what you need to know, how to go about it and has the software which is free to download.

MP3 software

ow that you've filled your hard drive with MP3 files, you'll need something to play them. Fact is, you probably already have a suitable piece of software. MP3s will play just fine with Windows Media Player on the PC and QuickTime's Movie Player on the Mac.

However, most people who get into MP3s prefer a dedicated MP3 player and there are several to chose from. Most are free, shareware or cost relatively little and even the ones which cost have a demo version so you can try them all and pick the one you like the best.

When investigating MP3 players you need to decide what features are important to you. As well as playing MP3 files, of course, a player might support other audio formats, have EQ controls (most do), and support skins which let you change the software's appearance. You will certainly want a playlist and maybe the ability to randomise a selection or search your hard disk for media files.

Some programs can encode MP3 files from Wave files, convert MP3s back to Wave files for burning to CD, and rip tracks from audio CDs which is obviously useful. We look at this aspect of MP3 in Chapter 8 but there are lots of CD rippers and MP3 encoders around so these features don't have to be on the top of your priority list.

MP3 players can have all sorts of other features, too. Many can play an audio CD, some produce graphic displays – eye candy – while playing the music, and some support plug-ins which give the program extra features such as playing other audio formats, adding effects or generating graphics.

Many of those which can play audio CDs support the CDDB (CD Database), an on-line resource of CD information. The first time you pop a CD in the drive the player connects to the CDDB and gets the album name, artist and track titles which it stores for future reference, saving you typing in all the info.

Insidious installations

Before we get to the players themselves, spare a thought about details you may be asked for before downloading or while installing the software. Some sites will not let you download software unless you provide an email address. Hint – this does not have to be a genuine address but some systems do check for the @ sign so gobbledygook may not be accepted whereas gobbledygook@hotmail.com will.

Also, some software virtually forces you to register over the Internet before it will launch the program. Again, you can use a false email address but make sure it doesn't pick up your address from your email software. The other option is to force quit the program at that point and then you can probably launch it without registering.

The players

WinAmp (PC) www.winamp.com

This is the world's favourite MP3 player, Figure 6.1, and for free it can't be beaten. It's packed with features such as EQ, a playlist, and it has a mini browser for seeking out MP3s when you're on-line. It supports audio CDs, additional audio formats and boasts an unbelievable 10,000 skins and 150 audio visualisation and effect plug-ins. Try this first and then compare the rest... However, those who like straightforward applications may find the interface and controls a little wee and dinky.

Sonique (PC) www.sonique.com

Arguably the world's second favourite MP3 player, Figure 6.2, and also free, although its dynamic windowless interface is not to everyone's taste. It's very much a personal thing. However, it's extremely well-featured with support for audio CDs, Windows Media files, Wave and other audio formats. It has a playlist editor, EQ, and it supports skins and plug-ins. There is a lot of support for it on the Web site.

False info – why?

If you've ever been on the receiving end of spam – and if you haven't you probably haven't used your email address yet! – you'll know why. Don't put any company past selling your email address, regardless of what their 'privacy policy' might say. One well-known developer of player software was caught out using their software to send them information about users' systems. Very naughty. You take care out there.

INFO

If you're a WinAmp user, here's a must-see site: www.1001winampskins.com

Figure 6.1(left): WinAmp – the most popular MP3 player in the world. Probably.

Figure 6.2 (right): Sonique – great features but the windowless interface will not be everyone's bag of bonios.

MusicMatch Jukebox (PC and Mac)

A large 7+Mb download gets you a highly functional program with CD ripping and CD burning, MP3 encoding, ID3 tag editing (more of this a little later), plug-in visualisations, links to the most popular music on-line, download recommendations, and more. The Mac version is new and has slightly fewer features. Jukebox used to be shareware but now it's free although you are encouraged to buy the MusicMatch Jukebox Plus version which rips faster, burns CDs faster, allows you to print your own CD covers with original album art and track info, and preset EQ settings.

Earjam ((PC) www.earjam.com

A free, well-featured player with support for all the popular audio formats, streaming audio, full screen video support, visual effects, third-party plug-ins, a music jukebox, CD burning and ripping, and it collects free music from EMusic.com. There is also a commercial Deluxe version with better sound quality (which sort of says that the free version is not the best quality so why bother...?), graphic EQ, unlimited MP3 encoding. But it looks nice.

RealPlayer and RealJukebox (PC) www.real.com

We've mentioned RealPlayer in previous chapters. It's the standard player for playing audio and video RealMedia files and it has built-in functions for seeking and playing streaming media from Internet radio, for example, although many other players do all this, too. It's probably a good idea to put the latest version of the RealPlayer on your PC. If you like it you can pay to upgrade to RealPlayer Plus. RealJukebox offers, er, jukebox facilities for playing and organising audio files, it can convert CDs to MP3 (more of this in Chapter 8), it includes animations, video, visualisations and it has a crossfade function. You can also pay to upgrade this to RealJukebox Plus.

PCDJ Broadcaster (PC) www.visiosonic.com

A novel MP3 player aimed at the aspiring DJ. As well as playing MP3 and other audio files, and ripping audio CDs, it can play and mix two audio or video files at the same time. It's free. Check it out.

UltraPlayer (PC) www.ultraplayer.com

Plays all popular audio formats, audio CDs and videos. It has an EQ section, supports skins – UltraSkins, actually – effects plug-ins, it can save MP3s as Wave files, and it has an alarm clock. The interface is a bit non-intuitive but then that's the way it is with many MP3 players.

Audion (Mac) www.panic.com

Well-featured and smart-looking player supporting the major audio formats. It has EQ with presets, playlist organisation, ID3 tag editor, some interesting skins, a karaoke mode for removing the vocals (this doesn't always work) if that's your thing, and an alarm clock. But it's not free, alas. It times out after 15 days unless you pay although it doesn't cost much.

Media Jukebox (PC) www.musicex.com
It supports over 20 media formats and burns audio CDs from over a dozen formats. It has EQ, a jukebox, it can encode MP3s, helps record vinyl and tape albums to disk, it has good search facilities for files and radio stations and a Top 40 function that tracks the most popular songs. It supports several portable players (more about these in the next chapter) and it has over 300 skins and supports WinAmp skins.

SoundApp (Mac) www.cs-students.stanford.edu/~franke/SoundApp
An audio file player and converter, it supports playlists and has a random shuffle mode.

SoundJam MP (Mac) www.soundjam.com
SoundJam MP Plus is a commercial MP3 player, widely regarded as one of the best with features falling out of its ears. You can download the free SoundJam MP player which has EQ, a playlist and an ID3 editor and get all the features of its big brother such as encoding, a playlist composer and an alarm clock for a 14 day trial period.

MacAst www.macast.com
Originally known as MacAmp, MacAst plays a range of audio formats, it can play audio CDs and streaming audio and it has custom skins. Also check out MacAst Lite which looks like the Mac's Control Strip but with EQ, and ID tag editor and skins.

Other MP3 player sites
We don't have room to list all the MP3 players out there but here are some other sites you might want to explore:

WPlay Pro (PC): www.mp3rulz.com
QuickAmp (Mac): http://homepage.mac.com/gtijerino/index.html
Soritong (PC): www.soritong.com
K-Jofol (PC): www.kjofol.org
GrayAmp (Mac): www.digithought.net
Destiny Media Player (PC and Mac): www.radiodestiny.com
AudioCatalyst (PC and Mac): www.xingtech.com
Baytex Party Pro (Mac): www.baytex.net

Figure 6.3: You don't have to be able to pronounce it, just admire the shapely curves of K-Jofol.

Figure 6.4 : GrayAmp –
it's gray (as they spell it
in America), it plays MP3s
and it's for the Mac.

MP3 software lists

Here are sites with links to MP3 software:

> *http://software.mp3.com/software*
> *www.mpeg.org/MPEG/MPEG-audio-player.html*
> *www.excite.com/entertainment/music/mp3/mp3_software/players*
> *www.mp3now.com/html/mp3_players.html*
> *www.audiovalley.com/mp3/mp3-software.html*
> *www.epinions.com/cmsw-MP3-All-Players*
> *www.sycast.com/therockwarehouse/trwmp3.html*
> *http://showcase.netins.net/web/phdss/mp3/mp3_players.htm*

MP3 utilities

Some MP3 players have a host of built-in features but there are also
a few specialist programs worth investigating.

Voquette Media Manager (PC) www.voquette.com
An intriguing piece of software which can play all popular forms of
downloadable audio such as MP3, RealAudio, Windows Media
Player, Wave files and streaming MP3s – yes, interesting, eh... It can
save recordings to hard disk or certain portable MP3 players, and rip
from audio CDs, too.

Lava (PC) www.lava.com
An interesting MP3 player which allows you to generate 3D graphics
to accompany the audio.

Netsonic Internet Accelerator (PC) www.netsonic.com
A utility designed to speed up Internet downloads – including MP3
files – by clever caching. It's free and there is a Pro version with
more features.

MP3Trim (PC) www.logiccell.com/~mp3trim
Cleans up and removes unwanted parts of MP3s. It can also amplify
and fade MP3s in and out.

INFO

Caching – a process
which stores or collects
information which may be
required before it actually
is required, which can
speed up transfer
operations.

Figure 6.4: Edit otherwise
uneditable MP3s with
MP3Trim.

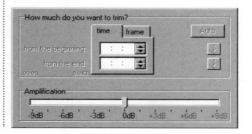

Changing your default MP3 player

When you start experimenting with MP3 players you'll find that many of them automatically assign MP3 files – and any other audio files they support – to themselves so when you double-click on an MP3 file, the application opens and plays it. That's fine but you may not want all audio files assigned to an application – you may prefer Wave files to open in an audio editor, for example – or you might decide you want to keep some earlier software as your main MP3 player. The solution is to reassign files to your preferred application.

To do this, find a file in Windows Explore, click on it to highlight it then hold down the Shift key and right-click on it. The resulting pop-up menu will contain an 'Open with...' option. Select it and a window will open listing the software installed on your PC. Select your preferred player and check the 'Always use this program to open this type of file' box. If the player isn't listed here, click on the Other button and navigate to the required application.

ID3 tags

After playing a few MP3 files, you'll notice that the MP3 player often displays not only the track name but artist and maybe album information, too. This data is embedded in the MP3 file in what is known as an ID3 tag. Many players can display this information and even allow you to edit it. This allows you to create your own ID3 tags of material you convert to MP3 format.

The original ID3 tag is limited to 128 bytes and is placed at the end of a file so the data will not appear at the start of playback with streamed files.

ID3v2 is a more flexible system which can be up to 256Mb in size – yes, it's big! – and is placed at the start of the file so streaming systems can use it. It also has a feature to prevent players which cannot read ID3v2 tags from trying to play the data. The size of the tag allows song lyrics, album cover artwork and even videos to be embedded in the data.

It also has a neat feature called the Popularimeter which can be used to count the number of times a file is played. This is intended to sort the good files from the bad and could be used to construct personalised playlists. It doesn't seem to have much support yet but give it time.

TIP

When installing a new player, if it gives you the option to select the files which will be associated with it, either deselect them all or just select the MP3 files. That way it's easier to revert to your previous settings if you need to.

INFO

You can find out more about the ID3v2 standard at:
www.id3v2.org

7

MP3 hardware

Because MP3 files are so small, lots of them can be stored in a few megabytes of RAM. It's not practical to carry a laptop computer around just to listen to MP3s but it is practical to store them in a RAM chip and carry that around. Add a pair of headphones and you've got a hand-held MP3 player.

Looking for a hand-held

There are several features to consider in an MP3 player. It's the usual trade-off between price and performance but use the following as a check list.

Style

Yes, the MP3 player you're carrying says a lot about you... Take a look at a few and you'll realise that style is important. But don't forget ergonomics and functionality.

Controls

Some players have spotty, closely-spaced buttons which can only be operated by three-year old fingers. If you're over three you want big buttons which are easy to find and operate. You'll want fast forward and rewind controls, but maybe also shuffle, repeat and skip functions, and an A-B repeat function which lets you mark a section to be automatically repeated.

Remote control

This is what you'll fiddle with while the player itself lies snugly in your pocket. Again, ease of use and ergonomics are of prime importance. Check that it has a clip for clipping onto your lapel.

Earphones

Most earphones simply plug into your ears and consequently tend to drop out when jogging or running for the train. A more robust option is backloop phones which clip around the back of your ears making them more stable.

Memory

The biggest consideration here is the size. Most players come with anything from 8-96Mb of built-in memory. You really need 64Mb to store a CD's worth of music so do your own sums. However, you can usually add more memory via SmartMedia cards so check this option to see how much can be added. Some can't take the larger 64Mb cards, for example, and don't be surprised to see 96Mb, 128Mb and 256Mb cards appearing.

LCD display

Most players now show track number and elapsed time (some cheapos may not) but what you really want is a display to show the track titles, artist and album name. Yes you do.

Sound quality

Well, some players do sound better than others but you can fiddle with the sound if the player has EQ controls.

EQ controls

Most players have a few EQ presets which can improve the sound, particularly important as you'll be listening on headphones which are not renowned for their good bass response. Some players have configurable EQ controls for those who like to fiddle.

Internal mic

A useful extra if you're prone to walking around talking to yourself – you can always pretend you were dictating notes into your MP3 player.

Phone book

Yes, some players can store phone details, too.

Interface

This is how the player connects to your computer and it's likely to be via the parallel (printer) port or USB. USB is easier and faster and the one you want, apart from being the only option for Mac users. PC users make sure your PC has a USB port...

Software

The main software is used to transfer MP3s from your PC to the player. If you're a Mac user, make sure the player has Mac software – alas, not all do. Most (but not all) software is easy to use. Some allow MP3s to be transferred from the player to the PC although many recent programs support copy restrictions which do not allow a file to be copied if it has been marked not eligible for copying.

The pack may also include a jukebox or computer-based player of some sort, maybe with the option to convert Waves to MP3s and vice versa. There is lots of software of this type around anyway (see Chapters 6 and 8) so this may not be a major consideration.

Extras

You may think you just want a player which plays back MP3s – but you don't. At least not if you want to be cool. Check out features such as Bookmarks which let you save several positions while listening, and then instantly go to any one of them; a browser for selecting tracks; a playlist editor; and a quick erase feature to delete unwanted tracks.

Specialist players

You know what's wrong with MP3s – you can't fill a CD with them and pop it into your CD player. At least you couldn't before but you can now with integrated CD/MP3 players. Essentially, all that needs to be done is to include MP3 decoding software and a few companies have already done it. Here's a few portable CD/MP3 players to look at.

Tagram's Mambo X www.mambox.com
CD-RW compatible and includes an infra red remote control.

Pine Technology's SM-200C www.pineusa.com
Can read VBR recordings, supports CD-RW, and includes an FM radio.

Easybuy 2000's MPTrip Discman www.easybuy2000.com
Reads CD-RW discs and has a built-in recharger for Ni-Cad batteries.

Adam Electronics' Adam MP3/CD/VCD Walkman www.adamelectronics.com
That's a name and a half but it tells you what it does. You can

> **INFO**
>
> MP3 players are smaller and lighter than portable CD or MiniDisc players and you can load whatever songs you want into them.

squeeze up to 200 tracks onto a CD, space permitting.

Philips' eXpanium www.expanium.philips.com
CD-RW compatible and the batteries should last for ten hours. Other combined and integrated MP3 players are also appearing.

Scan SC-2000 www.scan.co.uk
This is actually a DVD/MP3 player but you can see where it's all heading.

Hango Personal Jukebox www.pjbox.co.uk
This is a palm-sized player incorporating a 4.8Gb hard drive which can store over 80 hours of music at near CD quality. Connect it to your PC via USB and its software will automatically convert and download any CDs you put into your PC's CD ROM drive.

Webtronic's Webrome www.webtronicwarehouse.com
An interesting MP3 player shaped like a tape cassette. Pop it into a cassette player and it will play the MP3 files through the deck. An easy way to play MP3s on your car cassette player.

Samsung's SGH-M100 www.samsung.com
This is a cellphone. Yes, but it can also play MP3s! If you get a call, it pauses playback and displays the number so you can take the call or divert it. Hmm...

Transferring songs to an MP3 player

To illustrate the process of transferring files to an MP3 player, we'll use Samsung's Yepp, Figure 7.1, as an example. It comes with file management software called Yepp Explorer which is very easy to use. Plug the player into the PC via USB and the software will tell you when it recognises it because USB can do smart things like that.

The Yepp has built-in Flash memory which can be expanded with a SmartMedia card, and Yepp Explorer shows the contents of both memory areas. If you select Copy to Flash Memory from the File menu, Figure 7.2, a file dialogue box opens allowing you to select the files you want to load into the player. Alternatively, you can drag and drop files from Windows Explorer into the Yepp Explorer.

The Process Status area, bottom right, changes colour as loading progresses and the bottom of the window shows the number of files being loaded (here 5 of 9). The files and various file attributes are shown in the lower part of the window, Figure 7.3.

After all files have been loaded, they are listed in the Flash Memory window. The lower part of the window shows how many files there are and how much free space is left, Figure 7.4.

You can then disconnect the Yepp – you don't need to power

Figure 7.1: Samsung's Yepp, a rather neat MP3 player swamped by a lurid background.

Figure 7.2 (top left): Loading files into the Yepp's Flash memory.

Figure 7.3 (top right): The Yepp Explorer keep you informed about progress as file loading takes place.

Figure 7.4 (lower left): The lower part of the windows shows the total space and the amount of file space left.

Figure 7.5 (lower right): You can also transfer files from the Yepp back to the PC.

down or reset anything with USB – and play the files. You can transfer files back to the PC by right-clicking on a file and selecting Copy to PC from the pop-up menu, Figure 7.5. This will only work, however, if the file has not been tagged to prevent copying. Most free files available on the Internet will transfer back okay.

The Yepp also includes RealJukebox software, which can be used to organise and play your MP3s on your PC as well as other neat things such as playing audio CDs, getting track titles from the CDDB, recording CDs to disk, and creating custom playlists.

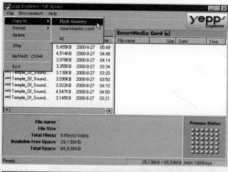

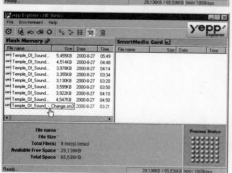

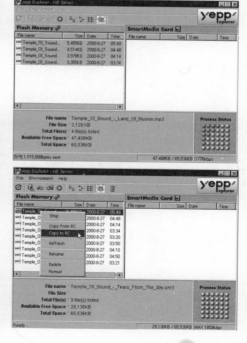

8

Creating your own MP3s

Now we get to the real fun part of MP3s – creating your own. There are two things you're likely to want to do. One is to convert audio CDs into MP3s and possibly tape or vinyl recordings, too. The other is to convert MP3 files into Wave files so you can burn audio CDs. Many people do this so they can play songs in the car. Just be aware that MP3 is a lossy compression system and converting MP3s to Wave files will still only give you the quality of the original MP3 file.

MP3 encoding

We've already seen that many MP3 players include MP3 encoding and if you already have one it's worth trying it first. Otherwise there are several freeware, shareware and commercial programs to choose from.

Traditionally, converting CDs to MP3 files is a two-stage process – you rip the audio from the CD in Wave format and then convert it to MP3. However, much software can now do the job in one go – you pop in the CD and the software converts the tracks directly to MP3s.

One such program is RealJukebox. Pop a CD in the drive, select Play/Record CD, click on the Record button and the program will play the CD while recording the tracks to your hard disk, Figure 8.1. However, the best conversion it can perform is 96kbps which may be fine for some folks but not good enough for others.

It can use error correction to improve the audio ripping and it will run a test on your CD drive to determine the best method of audio extraction.

MusicMatch Jukebox, offers similar automatic conversion facilities but you can choose a recording quality from 64kbps up to 160kbps. It has an option to use digital error correction during

INFO

There's more information about the best MP3 conversion settings to use in Chapter 2.

Figure 8.1 RealJukebox can play a CD while converting its tracks to MP3 files.

extraction which may improve recordings from a CD drive (or it may not) plus options such as VBR and CBR settings.

PCDJ Broadcaster can also rip audio CDs, offering conversion to Wave or WMA (Windows Media Audio) formats at up to 160kbps. It also has a jitter correction feature to help improve dodgy conversions from suspect CD ROM drives. Files can be loaded into Player A or B and you can do your DJ thing by mixing and crossfading between them. Okay, so these aren't MP3 files but most MP3 players can play them and if you need MP3 files, there are many utilities which can do the conversion.

Dedicated audio rippers and MP3 encoders

If you're messin' with just a few files, a combined MP3 player/encoder/CD ripper is probably the best solution, but if you're doing a lot of encoding it may be better to use dedicated software. There will be fewer distractions and it may have extra features such as batch conversion and it may encode higher bit rates than some MP3 players.

It will come as no surprise to learn that there are dozens of audio rippers and MP3 converters on the Web. Rather than try to list them all, we'll list a few sites which list them all; that way you can be sure of up-to-date information about the latest software available. Also check the list of codec sites in Chapter 2.

You'll find that many of these sites also list MP3 decoders which

http://showcase.netins.net/web/phdss/mp3/mp3_encoders.htm
www.mp3-it.com/software_encoders.html
www.mp3park.com/soft_encoders.html
www.maz-sound.com/mp3_text_only.html
http://dailymp3.com/encoders.html
www.mp3place.com/encoders.shtml
www.slaughterhouse.com/mp3encode.html

convert MP3s back into Wave files although, again, many MP3 players can do this, too, so you won't be short of options.

Bearing in mind what we said about the various MP3 codecs in Chapter 2, free software is unlikely to use the Fraunhofer codec (at least not legally) so you might want to try a few encoders to see what you think of the quality.

INFO

DirectX – a plug-in format which allows third-party effects ranging from specialist EQs to audio processing, to be added to a piece of software. All the major sequencers and editors support it. Although most major DirectX plug-ins are commercial, there are now hundreds of freeware and shareware plug-ins on the Net. For more information about DirectX plug-ins surf to: www.thedirectxfiles.com

Commercial MP3 software

There are also many commercial programs which can encode MP3s, rip audio from CDs, convert MP3s back into Wave files and burn them to CD, and most are relatively inexpensive.

You could check out the eJay MP3 Station Plus (www.fasttrak. co.uk) (there's no 'c' in 'fasttrak') which is part of the Dance eJay series. It actually integrates with the eJay 2 software to convert the Wave files they produce to MP3s but it also works as a standalone program to convert between MP3s and Wave files.

Magix's MP3 Maker (www.magix.com) can convert CD tracks to MP3, WMA and Wave files. It includes a Wave editor for trimming audio files and removing noise and clicks, useful for converting vinyl recordings to hard disk. The editor has lots of other functions, too, such as EQ, compression, time-stretching, fades and effects, and the program supports DirectX plug-ins which is unusual in such low-cost software. And for DJ wannabes, it can play two audio files at the same time while you crossfade between them.

Cakewalk Pyro (www.cakewlak.com) is yet another program which rips to MP3, Wave and WMA formats. It has a jukebox feature, it includes effects, supports DirectX plug-ins, and can burn CDs. It also includes CD label design software.

MP3 encoding on the Mac

Mac users can rip audio CDs using QuickTime and Movie Player. The interesting thing is, many Mac-based MP3 players tap into this audio extraction function of QuickTime and use their own front-end to offer easier access to the same conversion functions. This doesn't create an MP3 file but, again, you can convert it to MP3 using various utilities. SoundJam, for example, can rip audio tracks and convert them to AIFF, Wave, MP3 or MP2 formats. It offers conversion rates from 8kbps right up to 320kbps, and it has a range of additional encoder options.

Burning an audio CD from MP3 files

As mentioned earlier, to play a CD in a normal audio CD player, it must be written in 'audio CD' format. The usual process is to convert the files to Wave (or AIFF format on the Mac) and then use CD burning software to compile an audio CD. As with CD-to-MP3 ripping, some software can now do the MP3-to-Wave-to-CD conversion in one go on-the-fly which saves space as you don't have to store large Wave files prior to burning.

You need a CD-R, of course, and most of these come with CD burning software. On the PC, the most popular is Adaptec's Easy CD Creator (www.adaptec.com) and Ahead Software's Nero (www. ahead.de), while on the Mac it's Adaptec's Toast. In many cases these may be more flexible than using all-in-one MP3 ripper/player/burning software.

Ahead also has a dedicated audio CD burner called Feurio (www.feurio.com), which is shareware and undoubtedly one of the most comprehensive pieces of audio burning software yet to appear with audio ripping, CD Text, overburning, CDDB support, an audio editor and MP3 support, of course. It's got many advanced features so newcomers take it easy but if you do a lot of audio CD creation it's well worth downloading.

Track-at-Once vs Disc-at-Once

There are two methods of burning an audio CD. Tracks can be burned one at a time or the entire CD can be burned at once. With Track-at-Once (TAO) recording, the burning software includes a little bit of housekeeping data between the tracks. While such CDs should play okay on CD ROM drives, they may not play on standard audio CD players. TAO recording also limits the control you have over inter-track gaps.

With Disc-at-Once (DAO) recording the entire CD is burned in one go so there are no bits in between tracks to upset normal CD players, and you get more control over the inter-track gap. If possible, always use DAO when burning audio CDs.

Putting your music on the Web

If you're a musician, MP3s are a great way to distribute your music. The first thing many people think of doing is creating a Web site and putting their music there for visitors to download. This is certainly an option you should consider but the problem then is letting people know your web site exists and persuading them to visit it. Unless you already have a following this can be difficult.

A better idea, particularly for the newcomer, is to put your music on one of the 'band' sites we looked at in Chapter 4. These actively welcome new music and many pay a small fee each time one of your tunes is downloaded. Some will also burn a CD of your music, sell it on your behalf and share the proceeds with you.

Some sites have facilities for letting musicians create their own Web page.

INFO

CD Text – this incorporates track titles and artist information in the tracks which some modern audio CD players can display during playback.

INFO

Overburning – the art of squeezing more than 74 minutes of audio onto a CD. Not all CD-Rs or CD media support this.

How to get more downloads

When you put your music up on the Web you obviously want lots of people to download it. The best way to encourage people to do this is to keep the pieces short! Most people are still chugging along with 56K modems or slower and are more likely to download a small file than a large one. Whatever happened to artistic integrity, eh? But also remember that all sites stream files so visitors can tell if they want to download it so if the music is good, that obviously helps, too.

Appendix

MP3 music Web sites

www.amp3.com
www.ampcast.com
www.asiamix.com
www.audible.com
www.besonic.com
www.blindfrog.com
www.comedycircus.com
www.cybertropix.com
www.eatsleepmusic.com
www.eclassical.com
www.emusic.com
www.getoutthere.bt.com
www.getsigned.com
www.heardon.com
www.idnmusic.com
www.ihearyou.com
www.insound.com
www.jazzpromo.com
www.madasafish.com
www.mp3.com
www.mp3dd.net
www.mp3illusion.com
www.mp3miracle.com
www.mp3organized.com
www.musicblitz.com
www.musicmaker.com
www.peoplesound.com
www.riffage.com
www.tropia.com
www.tunes.com
www.vitaminic.co.uk
www.worldwidebands.
com

MP3 sharers, search engines and site listings

Napster
www.napster.com
Freenet
http://freenet.source
forge.net
Gnutella
http://gnutella.wego.com
Audiofind
www.audiofind.com
Audiophilez
www.audiophilez.com
AudioValley MP3 sites list
www.audiovalley.com
CuteMX
www.cutemx.com
Lycos
http://music.lycos.com
M-Music
www.m-music.net

MP3 Board
www.mp3board.com
MP3 Now
www.findsongs.com
MP3 Search
www.mp3search.nu
Palavista
www.palavista. com
Scour
www.scour.com
Spinfrenzy
www.spinfrenzy.com

MP3 software Web sites

Microsoft WMA
www.microsoft.com/win
dows/windowsmedia/en
/download/default.asp
WinAmp
www.winamp.com
Sonique
www.sonique.com
AudioCatalyst
www.xingtech.com
Audioactive Production
Studio
www. audioactive.com
MusicMatch Jukebox
www.musicmatch.com
RealJukebox
www.realjukebox.com
Audion
www.panic.com
N2MP3
www.n2mp3.com
Baytex Party Pro
www.baytex.net
MVP player
www.mvp.qdesign.com
SoundJam MP
www.soundjam.com
BladeEnc
http://bladeenc.mp3.no
LAME
www.sulaco.org
MP3Enc
www.opticom.de
MPegger
www.proteron.com/
mpegger
AT&T a2b
www.att.com/
campusalliance/
a2bmusic.html
www.a2bmusic.com
Liquid Audio
www.liquidaudio.com

Yamaha Sound VQ
www.yamaha-
xg.com/soundvq
CuteFTP
www.cuteftp.com
Fetch (FTP for Mac)
www.dartmouth.edu.
pages/softdev
Go!Zilla download
manager
www.gozilla.com
GetRight download
manager
www.getright.com
vTuner Internet radio
tuner
www.vtuner.com
Earth Tuner Internet radio
tuner
www.earthtuner.com
MacTuner Internet radio
tuner
www.aladdinsys.com
Voquette Media Manager
www.voquette.com
ShoutCast Internet radio
software
www.shoutcast.com
1001 WinAmp Skins
www.1001winamp
skins.com
Earjam player
www.earjam.com
RealPlayer
www.real.com
PCDJ Broadcaster
www.visiosonic.com
UltraPlayer
www.ultraplayer.com
Media Jukebox
www.musicex.com
SoundApp
www.cs-students.
stanford.edu/~franke/
SoundApp
MacAst
www.macast.com
WPlay Pro
www.mp3rulz.com
QuickAmp
http://homepage.mac.
com/gtijerino/index.html
Soritong
www.soritong.com
K-Jofol
www.kjofol.org

GrayAmp
www.digithought.net
Destiny Media Player
www.radiodestiny.com
Lava
www.lava.com
Netsonic
www.netsonic.com
MP3Trim
www.logiccell.com/
~mp3trim
Zlurp
www.zlurp.com

MP3 software lists

http://dailymp3.com/
encoders.html
http://showcase.netins.net
/web/phdss/mp3/mp3_
encoders.htm
http://showcase.netins.net
/web/phdss/mp3/mp3_
players.htm
http://software.mp3.com/
software
www.audiovalley.com/
mp3/mp3-
software.html
www.epinions.com/cmsw
-MP3-All-Players
www.excite.com/
entertainment/music/
mp3/mp3_software/
players
www.maz-sound.com/
mp3_text_only.html
www.mp3-it.com/
software_encoders.
html
www.mp3now.com/html/
mp3_players.html
www.mp3park.com/soft_
encoders.html
www.mp3place.com/
encoders.shtml
www.mpeg.org/MPEG/
MPEG-audio-player.
html

www.slaughterhouse.com
/mp3encode.html
www.sycast.com/therock
warehouse/trwmp3.html
www.media-island.com
www.maz-sound.com

Streaming audio software

www.hitsquad.com/smm/
cat/STREAMING_
AUDIO_MEDIA (note
upper case)

MP3 hardware Web sites

ABC MP3 Ltd
www.abcmp3ltd.co.uk
Adam Electronics
www.adamelectronics.
com
Audio Request
www.audiorequest.com
Casio
www.casio.com
Creative Labs
www.creative.com
Diamond
www.riohome.com
www.rioport.com
www.diamondmm.co.uk
Easybuy 2000
www.easybuy2000.com
JazPiper
www.jazpiper.co.uk
Empeg
www.empeg.com
Hango Personal Jukebox
www.pjbox.co.uk
LG Electronics
www.lge.com
MPMan
www.mpman.com
Philips
www.philips.com
www.philips.co.uk
Philips' eXpanium
www.expanium.philips.
com

Pine Technology
www.pineusa.com
Samsung
www.samsung
yepp.com
www.samsung.com
Scan
www.scan.co.uk
Schneider
www.schneider-ag.de
Tagram Mambo X
www.mambox.com
Thomson Lyra
www.thomson-
lyra.com
Vivanco
www.vivanco.de
Webtronic
www.webtronicware-
house.com

MP3 resources

Do MP3 encoders sound
different?
http://arstechnica.com/
wankerdesk/1q00/mp3/
mp3-1.html
Fraunhofer Institut
Integrierte Schaltungen
www.iis.fhg.de/amm
ID3v3 tags
www.id3v2.org
Manhattan Beach Music
Streaming audio primer
http://members.aol.com/
mbmband/html/
streaming.html
MPEG home page
www.cselt.it/mpeg
MPEG resources
www.mpeg.org
Record labels on the Web
www.rlabels.com
RIAA
www.riaa.com
Secure Digital Music
Initiative
www.sdmi.org

Index